F-CANCER

EUGENE BROOKS

Copyright © 2018 Eugene Brooks

All rights reserved.

ISBN: 978-0-692-19005-0

DEDICATION

I am dedicating this book to my longtime friend David Catoe who is still fighting Cancer. He gives me so much strength and hope watching him never give in to this disease. Love ya and keep fighting Dave. I also want to dedicate this book to my Mom and my two sisters, Regina and Raylene, who always picked up the phone and listened to me cry and complain. Most of all I want to thank Marian and my boys Matthew, Jacob, and Noah who had to live with me through this journey every day. To all the nurses at the VA Hospital in Houston, especially Nurse Jones and Nurse Brown, who carried me during those times that I was unable to carry myself. A big shout out to my ex-wife who housed me and went with me to all my appointments and was the first person there after my surgery. To my longtime friend Kimyatta Sanders who gave me much needed prayers and encouragement during the darkest of days. I wish my mentors Sammy G and Ron Simpson were still alive to see what they created. I think they would be proud of me. I love each and every one of you. THANK YOU!

FALLEN ANGEL

I am fallen,
But I am free,
I cannot fly, But I can see.
My soul is broken,
My body is cut,
But my heart is full,
Where my strength is not.
My wings may be torn,
My halo may be crooked,
But I have my friends,
Who will guide me when I
Am blinded.

"There is no table of contents dealing with Cancer; just a beginning and an end." — Eugene Brooks

Why am I my writing this book? Is it to fulfill some selfish need or am I trying to live up to a promise that I made with God during a time of desperation? Am I giving myself an additional layer of comfort by trying to help others, and define my purpose in life before Cancer rings its final bell? Emerson wrote, "The purpose of life is not to be happy, it is to be useful, to be honorable, to be compassionate, to have it make some difference that you have lived, and lived well."

Every Cancer patient faces some of the same concerns, thoughts, anxieties, and fears irrespective of the type of Cancer that they are battling. There is a certain language that Cancer patients use to communicate our fears, sorrow, pain, and hope with each other. There is always a need to find hope even if it's through another patient's sad story. This written conversation about my experiences and knowledge gained is an expression of hope to my brothers and sisters who are still fighting Cancer. I don't like to call the words etched on these papers a book. A book suggests a set of rules and guidelines that must be followed in the literary world. I would rather call these written words a conversation. I intend to talk to you, and not at you. I want it to feel like we are all sitting in a waiting room and we start sharing with each other our stories and experiences about our journey with Cancer. This is me telling my story. I have chosen not to follow any of the traditions that you would normally find in a book. It doesn't mean that my thoughts aren't organized, which has been doubted during my path with Cancer, it just means that I want these words to reflect the lack of organization that exists when fighting Cancer. Which is NONE!! There are no chapters, table of contents, commas where there should be or any other rules that you would traditionally find in a book. Yes, I did bend a little and included page numbers and there is a glossary of terms located in the rear of the book. I still do have my type A personality and still can be a bit OCD from time to time. LOL!!

What you will find in this conversation is my remarkable story of battling Cancer. While on this journey every rule was broken. There was nothing normal about the road that I have traveled so far dealing with this beast. I try and share my strength, hope, and knowledge gained through this process to help other Cancer patients who are still on the battlefield. I also want to share a different perspective that may help Cancer patients see the joy and love that is also present with Cancer. Living with Cancer is one of the most difficult things that I have been through in my life, and there have been many during my fifty plus years. Many people would consider that my life before Cancer had already been filled with enough life challenges. Before being diagnosed, I had experienced sexual abuse at a young age, an identity crisis (bi-racial), drug addiction, homelessness, and bouts of depression. I was able to survive all those obstacles, regain my footing in life, and eventually, work my ass off and earn a Bachelors Degree and a Law Degree. The difference between Cancer and all the other ill's that I have experienced is simple to explain. There has always been an answer before Cancer, and that answer has always been, to some degree, controlled by me. My life has been a series of lessons that I have learned over time. Some lessons more painful than others because in the past I was guided by my ego, stubbornness, and ignorance about a higher power. Each lesson built on the next lesson. All the previous lessons helped me survive and thrive through this crazy Cancer journey. I will get to the God element. Just hold on. I can't give you the whole book in the first couple of pages. LOL!!

Cancer is a different animal. It's an uncontrollable monster that seems never to have an end. You may be Cancer free for years, and then a simple check-up reveals that Cancer has resurfaced in all its ugly glory. My thoughts at times, I must admit, can be morbid and some would argue even pessimistic. I can assure you that those thoughts are housed with a great amount of faith and hope. I always remain a realist. It's very similar to that of John McCain. Senator McCain didn't give up his fight with Cancer when he elected to stop treatment. He knew that it was his time to exit off the highway of life. No one can tell me that his will had been broken. If his will to live couldn't be broken in Vietnam, nothing else in life had a chance. He came to a place of acceptance that it was his time. We will all have to take that exit while traveling through life. It's inevitable and its ahead of us all. Senator McCain understood that all that could have been done to extend his life was done. He was a realist and wasn't afraid of his transition. Realism and pessimism are two different things. Part of my answer to Cancer is dealing with the realities of this disease as honestly as possible. There is no good reason to sugar coat our reality. Most of us don't want pity. We hate to hear, "It's gonna be OK." We know that there is a possibility that it may not turn out the way we want. We just want the truth. How we receive that truth and process that truth is what's hard. My intention in my words is to help you grow with acceptance and to give you some tips that I used to process the truth healthily and happily to survive and live with a heart full of love through your travels with Cancer.

After being diagnosed, I wanted answers to some of my questions about what I was facing. I wanted to know more from people that had gone before me about what was in store for me as I faced those very difficult times in my life. I had no idea when I was diagnosed with Cancer what tests and treatment methods I was going to have to endure. Google with all its power didn't prepare me for the long periods of waiting and wondering what will happen to my boys and me. I wanted to hear from other patients about what I should expect when I was going to have a TACE procedure, heart catheterization, organ transplant, rounds of chemo, and the other tests needed to fight Cancer. It's so frightening going into those cold rooms laying on those tables with only your thoughts not knowing what to expect and how much discomfort I would have to endure. You must become an active participant in your healthcare. We have to become educated about our disease so we can see things clearly. Family members are also seeking answers about how to prepare for their future. I'm using the word future, but it's often defined in very short periods of time.

It truly is a one day at a time adventure. You loved ones are trying to figure out what tomorrow will be like after a full day of testing, chemo, radiation, transplant surgery or after getting more information about a condition.

My intentions and desires for writing this book are to try and explain, in a very honest way, how I have been able to survive all the medical shit and at the same time prepare to die with Cancer if that's what the outcome would have been for me. Relationships will be created, and old ones will have a chance of being strengthened or better yet revitalized. I have discovered that there is a spiritual, emotional and physical component to dealing with this entire process. The idea of death is not a new idea, and it's something that we will all have to come to terms with at some time in our life. Cancer just gives you a warning sign much like a street sign on a very dangerous road. If you take heed of that sign and slow down, you can prepare for the end of the road. The road can be a very frightful ride, or it can be much smoother even if it includes a few unexpected potholes and sudden turns. Any road trip is manageable when you have a map of the terrain. I intend to create a roadmap, so you don't fall off the cliff while on a dark road.

In the past, I was able to use my earlier struggles in life to help me navigate any challenge that life could possibly throw my way. There are certain principles and tools that I have been blessed to learn from my past experiences I MUST share. I use the word MUST because it is my reason for living. It's my sole purpose in life. This written conversation is me paying my promissory note to God. It's part of my destiny. This has always been my calling to share my thoughts through words with others who are searching for a way to battle and live with Cancer. I'm sure after reading about my battle with Cancer that it will be clear that I have a calling placed upon me. After many years I have come to accept all that is required of me by God. My message is not only for the patients but also for the caregivers and families. I tried many times to isolate those people from me as much as possible. I have also realized that those people who are on this journey with us have their own spiritual experience and we can't deny them this experience because it is an opportunity for them to learn spiritual lessons and gather tools for the rest of their journey. This Cancer/life thing is much bigger than me. This Cancer/life thing is not bigger than you and me together. Through faith and an optimistic approach, we can live and enjoy this time in our lives.

I would admit that the struggle to maintain that faith and optimism can at times require some work and care. It's very similar to a flower. You must feed and water that flower. It requires the right amount of sun to produce the food it needs to survive. Your thoughts control your attitude, your attitude controls how you will interpret the things that you will experience during your days. Those thoughts and the manner in which you care for them during this journey is what I want to share. My ability to dance with death while maintaining a smile seemed to others, who were watching me, like a wonderfully orchestrated ballad. It looked effortless. In reality, it required a lot of work. There were plenty of times that I was uncomfortable. Change is always uncomfortable, but with the right perspective, it doesn't have to be painful. It's because of this journey and encouragement from both friends and strangers that I am writing this book. I want to share the dance with Cancer that I had with other people that I am bonded with because of Cancer.

"The question is not how to get cured, but how to live."

— Joseph Conrad

I realized that this journey was about more than just living or dying of Cancer. It was complicated. There was a spiritual challenge that I had to grab and hold on to if I was going to make it. I needed to be educated about my disease, but I needed the spiritual side to bring balance to something that seemed so overwhelmingly not in my favor. I had always believed that everything in my life was controlled by God and I knew that this disease was a blessing. There was this really smart guy whose name was Albert Einstein who wrote," There are two ways to live your life.... One is as though nothing is a miracle; the other is as though everything is a miracle." This had been my mantra for 20 years before I was first diagnosed with Cancer. I had to choose a path to survive through this experience. I decided that this was going to be a spiritual experience and I promised myself that I was going to absorb all those daily miracles and embrace all the love that will shine on me. Remember, we are spiritual beings having a human experience. I would try and enjoy every smile and kind word and give it the depth and weight that it deserved. This is the time to see past the physical world. Every lesson that will be shown to me will be a guide. My friends, loved ones, and strangers will be my guiding light. I am truly the passenger on this spiritual ride. I am not the driver. Any little pieces of comfort and peace mean a lot while dealing with Cancer and waiting for a transplant. Giving people the opportunity to help you is a blessing. It's a blessing for the patient that he has people to help him.

The other issue that seems to be one of the hardest for a lot of people today is patience. Our society has been trained to want everything, and they want everything right now!! We are a society that is built on instant gratification. Waiting is always difficult. We usually find it hard to wait for the work week to end. Now imagine waiting for your life to be saved. It's very intense and scary. It's crucial that you find a way to cope with the stress and anxiety of waiting. You're trying your best to maintain some type of normal life and do the things that you did in the past while waiting. We usually know what we are waiting for, but with Cancer, we are totally clueless. I finally decided to accept that I have a new normal. Enough about focusing on the end. I had to focus on living. Stay living in the light of hope.

Prayer was something that I relied on every day. People would always tell me that I must ask God for a liver and that he would answer my prayers. I could never pray to God asking for a liver. I thought it was very selfish besides just not being very realistic. I could pray a thousand times a day for me to hit the lottery, and I knew that it would not have any impact on me being a Powerball winner. I mean really!! C'mon. How could I ask God to take a person's life, so I could live? That's just a bit too selfish for me. I can't hope that some family will be in pain so mine can be happy. I only asked God for his Will to be done. I prayed and asked that he give me acceptance. I asked that he gives me comfort accepting his Will for me. The serenity prayer was the prayer that got repeated many times during the journey. God grant me the serenity to Accept the things I cannot change, the courage to change the things I can, and the wisdom to know the difference. There is also a short version for this prayer that I used from time to time, "Fuck it."

Life is a journey. When we stop, things don't go right.

-Pope Francis

I was diagnosed August 16, 2013, with Hepatocellular Carcinoma (HCC), commonly referred to by layman as just Liver Cancer. They discovered two lesions at the dome of the liver on segment 5 of the right lobe. A simple tumor marker blood test called AFP (*see terms*) confirmed their diagnosis. This is a blood test to look for alpha-fetoprotein (AFP) in your blood. AFP is one of several tumor markers that help doctors diagnose liver disease. Tumor markers are molecules in the blood that are higher when a person has certain cancers. AFP is found mainly in liver cancer. The liver Cancer was not a big surprise because for the previous 20 years I had been fighting Hep C. The progression was something that Dr's had warned me about while I was getting treatment for Hep C. I tried every treatment available for Hep C that was available during those twenty years. I was treated with Interferon, Interferon with Ribavirin twice, and a slew of homeopathic herbs and vitamins. I always knew that if a scientist didn't find a cure that it would ultimately lead to this point in my life. As luck would have it, after I was diagnosed with Cancer, a cure was finally found for this disease. They now have a drug called – Harvoni that is quite successful in curing Hep C. I was placed on Harvoni, and after a couple of months my Hep C was arrested and cured. It was too late for my liver, and the damage could not be reversed. At least my new liver wouldn't be attacked and damaged by the

Hep C virus. The only chance for me to survive this Cancer would be to have a Liver Transplant (*see terms*).

All my treatment during this period was being handled at the Michael E. DeBakey VA Medical Center in Houston. The VA does a phenomenal job, despite some of the things that you hear on the news, at making sure that vets are kept on a strict routine of preventive care. Because of the strict routine and my history with Hep C, my Cancer was caught early. Anyone will tell you that the earlier you catch Cancer, the better your chance of survival. After being diagnosed with Cancer, I was referred to the liver transplant team at the hospital to start the evaluation process to determine if I was a good candidate for transplantation. At any transplant program the key person, even before the surgeons, is your transplant coordinator. He or she will be the person to guide you through the entire process, before and after transplantation. You will have a long relationship with that person so try to be nice. I was very fortunate to have the best in the business to lead me through this process. The transplant coordinators at the VA hospital in Houston are Nurse Jones and Nurse Brown. I would advise anybody that if you are going through this process that you try your best and create a good relationship with them. Make sure you have your coordinator firmly on your side. Whatever he or she asked you to do you should comply completely with their orders. I got the best of both worlds with Jones and Brown. One had a very soft ear and the other a very honest tongue. Nurse Brown just exudes love and understanding. Brown is like your mother and Jones is like your big sister. Momma is going to love you and console you through everything. Now, she will get in your butt and correct you, but in a nice kinda way. Jones reminds me of your big sister. She is going to protect you against others until you get alone and then she is gonna let you have it. Nurse Brown will give you a very soft version of the truth. There are times when a soft version is what we seek and need. Remember, we won't be at our strongest every day. Now Jones is going to give you the truth a little bit differently. Which I needed most of the time. I like to deal with the facts, no matter what they are. Veterans are a unique group of patients. Keep in mind that many of these individuals have been in harm's way and are very headstrong. Not all of them of course, but many of them require a strong hand and even a stronger leader. Nurse Jones was a veteran and has had years of experience dealing with men who think that they are superior to women. So, she was well equipped to deal with veterans at the hospital. Jones was the person I went to when I just needed someone to give me the bottom line. Don't bullshit me and try to sugar coat the issue.

My first introduction to Nurse Jones was memorable. It happened a couple of weeks before my first scheduled appointment with the transplant team. I had an appointment to meet with a physician's assistant who was tasked with the job of giving me an outline of the process that I was about to begin to get a new liver. God sure does have a way of doing things. At the appointment, the lady at the desk who checks you in for your appointment was a bit abrasive and rude to me, and to other veterans who had appointments that day. I usually find myself to be the defender of other people that may not be able to adequately defend themselves. I got into a little argument with the lady about her attitude and her not respecting veterans in the waiting room. Well, guess who happened to be right down the hallway and overheard the argument. Yep, Nurse Jones. Because Nurse Jones is very respected by her colleagues and is the coordinator of the transplant program, she has a great deal of influence in the hospital. Nurse Jones told me that I cannot be so combative with the staff and I needed to follow directions. I was trying to explain to Nurse Jones, in my condescending way, that it was not me that had the attitude and was starting the confusion. Well, that didn't go well, and Nurse Jones and I kinda exchanged a few words. The attitude of the woman that morning wasn't anything new that I had experienced. There are times that quite a few employees at the VA address veterans in a very demeaning tone. There are some issues that the VA needs to be addressed just like any other large healthcare institution. The attitude towards veterans is the one major issue that I have seen and experienced while going to the VA hospital. I have on several occasions had to demand that I be treated with respect and not be made to feel as if I was getting something for free. It feels as if the staff thinks that you should be grateful that you are receiving any care at all. If you have never been to a free clinic or county hospital, you might not understand the look in a person's eye when they are talking down to you instead of talking to you. I don't want you to think that I am saying every employee at the VA conducts themselves in this manner. I am the first one to tell a veteran that they should go to the VA for their healthcare if they have served. This was one of those times that the women had crossed the line. I often would have to remind the staff who have crossed that line that I had both a Bachelors Degree and a Law Degree. This attitude of thinking that all vets are beneath them is not only present in some of the staff, but also with some of the doctors. Again, you must remember the VA is the largest healthcare provider here in the United States so there will always be room for improvement. Ok, got that off my chest. I might have been a little short that morning, to be honest, but she still deserved to be put in her place. After exchanging a few choices words with Nurse Jones, I sat back down and waited for my appointment. The physician assistant that was doing the initial evaluation told me that I needed to get along with everyone and especially Nurse Jones because she was going to be your transplant coordinator. Shit!! Shit!! Shit!! This is going to be a long process, I thought in my mind. That ended up not being the case at all. Nurse Jones ended up being my angel. In time Nurse Jones and I became very close, and Jones became my greatest advocate. The incident with Jones was just Nurse Jones being Nurse Jones. She is a protector and the greatest ally you could possibly have on your side. As I said earlier, she is a vet herself and understands what it is like to be a vet. She knows that some vets are just special and require a different type of care. I wouldn't be surprised that after that dispute with that rude ass lady Nurse Jones pulled her to the side and counseled her about her behavior. I don't know if it happened, but I wouldn't be surprised. I learned that day if I had any problems while at the VA I knew who I needed to have on my side. I might be a little slow at times, but I ain't no fool. This fight we are in is not a game. Figure out your way of being successful, your life depends on it. Find the leader and attach yourself to that person. I also knew I had to redeem myself and be the very best patient that she has ever served. She wasn't gonna have any more problems out of Eugene Brooks. Well, that's what I promised myself that day, and for the most part, it was true. I may have swayed away occasionally, but I still believe that I have, and still am, her favorite patient. Ok maybe that was my ego typing that line, but we gonna run with it. LOL !!

After my introduction to Nurse Jones, I was a bit concerned, and I started doing some research on the VA and their liver transplant team. Boy was I surprised at what I discovered. The survival rates for patients receiving liver transplants at the Michael E. DeBakey VA Medical Center surpassed national averages. According to a study the one-year patient survival rate is around 97.06 percent surpassed almost all other hospitals. The expected survival rate of 90.30 percent and the national hospital average of 89.53 percent. Please remember that it's important to do some research on your physicians and the hospital that will be caring for you. The VA transplant program cares for veterans not only in Texas but also from surrounding states. The VA pays for the transplant patients to be flown in for all the testing and on the day of the transplant. Also, they pay for the rooms and boarding for the patient and their caregiver. It's this type of information that the media doesn't report about the VA system.

> "I am not afraid to die; I am only afraid of saying goodbye to you forever."
>
> — *Shannon L. Alder*

Every step in the process can be very stressful because you have now stepped into the unknown powerless zone. You are now officially powerless, and the clock has started to run. You have no control in deciding if you will be approved to be listed for a new liver. Just because the doctors have discovered that you need a new liver doesn't equate to you getting a new liver. All it means is that if you don't get a new liver the Cancerous liver will fail, and you will die. You are also not in control if you do get listed, or will you be able to stay in criteria until you transplant.

The transplant process is costly and takes a team of people working a lot of hours to pull this miracle together. Solid organ transplantation is one of the miracles of modern medicine. It is an effective and cost-effective therapy for people like me with end-stage organ failure, saving lives and improving the quality of patients' lives. Unfortunately, there are many insurance barriers that limit the success of transplantation in the US today. Start the process immediately with your insurance carrier so you will have one less thing hanging over your head. Transplantation is a treatment, not always a cure for end-stage organ failure. Transplant recipients will also be required to take immunosuppressive medications for their entire lives to prevent rejection which also is very expensive. Stopping these medications, for even a brief period of time, places us at high risk of rejection. These medications also have many potentially serious side effects. Thus, transplant recipients require ongoing monitoring and access to medical care for their entire life. Also, transplant patients often have many other medical problems and require multiple other medications as well. Unfortunately, many transplants fail due to patients' inability to afford necessary medications or other aspects of essential medical care. Another important barrier is the lack of insurance coverage, which prevents many patients with end-stage organ failure from even getting a transplant. This appears to be particularly evident for minority and lower socioeconomic populations. In determining if you will be a candidate for transplant all these variables are considered. It wouldn't be fair to allow money from keeping you from getting excellent care, but unfortunately, we live in a society that has not adopted a form of health care that works for all. We did make progress when President Obama was in office. Thanks to him we won't be denied coverage because of pre-existing conditions, and there is no cap on the amount of money that can be spent on your treatments before losing coverage. It's vital to your sanity that this is taking care of as soon as possible, so you have one less thing to stress about while going through this already taxing process. It's a pain in the ass so just get it over so you can plot a course for yourself.

One of the smartest things I did as soon as I was diagnosed with Cancer was to apply for Social Security Disability. I was being seen at the VA, so I didn't have the headache of dealing with the insurance companies, but I still wanted to have a backup plan in case something crazy happened, or if I just have one of those days and start cussing folks out. I know me, and I can have those moments when I don't always behave correctly. The normal process for getting approved for disability can usually take forever. There is a faster process for some patients if they have a certain disability. The Social Security agency created a list called Compassionate Allowance that speeds the process up. If you have a certain disease or disability and it is on the list, your application will be on a Fastrack and can be approved in days once you have all your documents together. You must know the exact name of your diagnosis, and then you can go online and check to see if it is on the list.

Ok, so now that the paperwork is being completed, we must go through the poking and prodding of our bodies. Most of the tests were relatively painless. The amount of time it took to complete the exams was the hardest part for me. The first day was very long. You're scheduled for quite a few of these tests in one day. They really try and get the assessment done as quickly as possible. I'll talk later about the importance of getting you on the list as quickly as possible. Make sure to take a book, laptop or something to keep you distracted. And I'm sure we all know that we should have something to keep us warm because it's always freakin cold in hospitals. Some of the tests that you will go through include a complete bone scan, X-ray, CT Scan (*see terms*) or MRI (*see terms*), Pet Scan (*see terms*), ultrasound, endoscopy (see terms), colonoscopy (*see terms*), echocardiogram, stress test, and maybe a cardiac catheterization (*see terms*) to determine the strength of your heart, colonoscopy (*see terms*), endless amounts of blood being drawn, and a psychological exam. The Doppler ultrasound test will determine if the blood vessels to and from the liver are open. Echocardiogram to help check the heart function. There will also be pulmonary function studies to determine the lungs' ability to exchange oxygen and carbon dioxide. Blood tests to determine blood type, clotting ability, the biochemical status of blood, testing to gauge liver function, HIV, hepatitis screening and other viral testing (Herpes and Epstein-Barr) are also included in the battery of tests. The psychological exam will include an assessment to determine if you have a support system to help you before and after transplantation, any issues with depression, financial abilities, suicidal tendencies, drug or alcohol addiction, and you must also demonstrate that you have a stable living environment. This is usually performed by a transplant social worker or psychologist. You will also meet with your transplant surgeon as part of your introduction to what was going to take place during your transplant. Dr. Cotton was the transplant surgeon that my caregiver and I met to give us information about what happens during the transplant surgery. There was no doubt that Dr. Cotton was a brilliant man and God built him to be a surgeon. He was a smaller man with these very soft nimble hands. They were just perfect for handling instruments and maneuvering inside your body. He was very compassionate and extremely engaging. He took the time to answer any questions that we had for him. It was a great experience, and I was very comfortable with him doing the surgery.

Quite often when you're going to have a bone scan, MRI or CT-Scan you must have to either drink some type of contrast or be injected with contrast and then wait an hour or two. Some require that you drink the contrast before going in and while on the table they will inject you with additional contrast. It's more stressful then painful. You do have this warm feeling, and you may think you're going to have a bowel movement on the table when they start the injection of the contrast. You won't, but it just feels that way. It does for me anyway. Any one of the results can be the thing that eliminates you from getting your transplant. It can be a lonely feeling laying on those cold ass tables, and this machine is just banging away getting the images that hold the key to your future. I was unable to complete an MRI because I'm claustrophobic. The tube for the MRI was just too small for me. I thought I was going to die in that tube. They do have open MRI machines available today because there is a large population of people who are unable to lay still in a closed MRI machine. The VA didn't have an open MRI, so all my scans were done using the CT scanner.

After a few weeks or so of going through all the paper work and testing, I was approved by UNOS to receive an organ transplant, and I was put on the waiting list. My initial MELD score was 20. This was the first hurdle that was cleared. You get a chance to exhale for a minute, and you should take that minute to decompress. While you're on this journey, it's important to take those small moments and relax for a couple of days. Remember it's a marathon, and there are quite a few hurdles that you will have to clear before getting to transplantation.

Ideas are easy. Execution is everything.

It takes a team to win.

- John Doerr

United Network for Organ Sharing (UNOS) is the private, non-profit organization that manages the nation's organ transplant system under contract with the federal government. UNOS manages the national transplant waiting list, matching donors to recipients 24 hours a day, 365 days a year. More than 120,000 people in the U.S. are waiting to receive a life-giving organ transplant. There are simply not enough donated organs to transplant everyone in need, so UNOS must balance the following factors when deciding who will receive that donated organ: justice (fair consideration of candidates' circumstances and medical needs), medical utility (trying to increase the number of transplants performed and the length of time patients and organs survive). Many factors used to match organs with patients in need are the same for all organs, but the system must accommodate some unique differences for each organ. Donated organs require special methods of preservation to keep them viable between the time of procurement and transplantation. Heart, lung: 4-6 hours, liver: 8-12 hours, pancreas: 12-18 hours, and kidney: 24-36 hours. The team must act swiftly to distribute those organs so make sure you are ready to go when they call.

Organs are distributed by UNOS throughout different

regions in the U.S. There are 11 different regions spread out through the United States. The distribution of organs is very complicated, and it's currently undergoing changes as I am writing this book. Many argue that some regions are transplanting much quicker and those patients in those regions are not as sick as other patients in different regions. An average Meld score in the western regions are much higher, and a patient in California will have to wait much longer than a patient in Texas. They must also consider the viability of those organs once extracted from the donor. The faster they get the organ out of the donor and into the patient the better the chances of success. So, the organs can't always be put on a plane and sent across the country. The expense is also considered when trying to be fair about organ distribution. It is permissible to register in several different regions to increase your chances of getting a transplant. If you have the money to travel that quickly, it's a great advantage. People have also moved to another region to increase their chances of survival. I guess if you have the means you can register in multiple regions if you can get on a plane at the drop of a dime and get to the hospital within hours after getting the call.

Here in the Southern region, the average MELD score at the time of transplantation is around 32. After doing some research after I was listed with UNOS, I figured out I was probably going to have to be on the wait list for about 2 years. I have a very common blood type of O+, so it was a good thing and a bad thing.

The criteria used for a liver transplant is not the same that's used for kidneys, lungs, hearts and other organs. An ALAS calculator is used for heart and lung transplantation, kidney/pancreas uses CPRA, and MELD is used for the liver and intestines. They will take certain tests scores and other variables to calculate a score to determine your position on the list. I mentioned earlier how important Nurse Coordinators are in your transplant process and the speed at which your application is processed is paramount. It literally can come down to seconds if you are selected to receive an organ that is available. If all things are equal, the person whose application was put in first will get that organ. At the VA those application packets are put together and submitted by Nurse Jones and Nurse Brown, who knows the importance of getting them submitted as quickly as possible.

The scoring criteria I will be discussing is specifically for liver transplantation. The Model End-Stage Liver Disease (MELD) scoring system that's used for liver transplantation is very complicated. They use your age, bilirubin (*see terms*), creatinine (*see terms*), INR (*see terms*), and serum sodium blood results to calculate a score ranging from 1 to 40. One being not sick at all to

40 which means you are gravely ill. Normally if your score is not at least a 10, you won't even be referred to a hepatologist and started on the process of transplantation. Based on my research and talking to a lot of transplant patients the average score for getting a liver is around 32-34 here in Texas and the data would suggest that the wait time is around 24-36 months. If you have a rare blood type once again that time frame could be shorter or longer.

Different types of liver diseases would warrant a transplant. So, depending on what type of Cancer you have there may be another criterion that will be between you and getting approved for a transplant. If you are diagnosed with Hepatocellular Carcinoma (HCC), which was the type of Cancer I had, they use the Milan Criteria. So, if you fall outside of this criterion, you will not remain on the list and will not keep getting points. You must remain in criteria. I know it's getting complicated now. Remember you have the MELD scoring system that determines your position on the list, and you also have another criterion that makes sure that your Cancer hasn't spread, or you have too many lesions. It again comes down to giving the organs to candidates who have the greatest chances of survival. They take the images from the CT-Scan or MRI to see how many lesions you have and where they are located. If your lesions get too large or if you have too many then they feel as if your chances of survival are not as great as others who are within criteria. The threshold Milan criteria are as follows: (1) you can have one lesion, and it must be smaller than 5 cm; alternatively, you can have up to 3 lesions, but each lesion must be smaller than 3 cm. (2) no extrahepatic manifestations. Extrahepatic manifestation means diseases or conditions that affect organs other than the liver. So, it can't have spread to other parts of the body. So plainly speaking you want to be sick to get points, but not too sick to be deactivated from the list.

Every three months you will be scanned to determine the size growth and placement of your tumors inside the liver. It's always stressful when you go in the hospital for another scan to determine if you are still within criteria. You're hoping the Cancer isn't spreading so you can keep gaining points while your MELD score keeps increasing. It can drive you crazy. If you fall outside of the criteria, you will not be eligible for a transplant, and if you have already been on the list your name will be removed or deactivated from the active donor recipient list. You can be reinstated on the list if they can get some of the lesions to decrease in size or eliminated altogether. The results of your scan every three months with your recent blood work will be sent to UNOS so you can be given the additional points you need. Initially you see increases normally of three points every three months. Once you get around 25 – 28 points those increases in your score will slow down. You may only get one point instead of the traditional three points. Again the increases will be calculated by UNOS based upon the formula we discussed earlier. MELD uses the patient's values for bilirubin, serum creatinine, and the INR. It is calculated according to the following formula: MELD = $3.78 \times \ln[\text{serum bilirubin (mg/dL)}] + 11.2 \times \ln[\text{INR}] + 9.57 \times \ln[\text{serum creatinine (mg/dL)}] + 6.43$. Don't worry about trying to do the calculations I just added that formula in the book for my fellow geeky people like me. You can go to google and search Meld Calculator and you will be able to find a site that has a calculator. If you have problems, I will have a calculator available on my site at fcancernow.com. All you have to do is insert your blood work numbers and it will do the calculations for you.

The only question that always haunted me was will I be able to maintain my health until I transplanted. Besides having a failing liver, I was also diabetic and had high blood pressure. I had both under control, so I didn't see those ailments as something that would keep me from the list, but it was just something else that was always in the back of my mind. Because of my liver disease, I also had another condition called Thrombocytopenia. The blood flow from my spleen was constricted, and my platelets were dying in my spleen.

Platelets keep you from bleeding to death if you are cut. A normal platelet count should be around 300 or higher. During this time my count was around 90. I was given medication for this condition to assist me in maintaining some type of blood flow so the platelets wouldn't die in the spleen. Again, it still was not an obstacle that would bar me from the list.

Another common issue that arises in patients with liver disease is ascites, and jaundice (*see terms*). Jaundice" is the medical term that describes yellowing of the skin and eyes. Jaundice itself is not a disease, but it is a symptom of several possible underlying illnesses. Jaundice forms when there is too much bilirubin in your system. Bilirubin is a yellow pigment that is created by the breakdown of dead red blood cells in the liver. Normally, the liver gets rid of bilirubin along with old red blood cells. This is why the results from this test are included in making up your MELD Score because it is an indicator of how well your liver is performing.

One of the other symptoms that generally occurs with liver disease is acsites. This was probably the only symptom that I didn't suffer from while waiting to transplant. The most common cause of ascites is liver cirrhosis. Other causes include cancer, heart failure, tuberculosis, pancreatitis, and blockage of the hepatic vein. In cirrhosis, the underlying mechanism involves high blood pressure in the portal system and dysfunction of blood vessels. The abdomen will increase in size because there is a buildup of fluids. You will have to decrease your salt intake, and they may also give you a diuretic. Sometimes fluids continue to build up in the abdomen despite the use of diuretics and a restricted salt diet. In these cases, patients may need paracentesis to remove this large amount of excess fluid. For the procedure, the patient's belly is cleaned and a local anesthetic is administered to numb the area. A long, thin needle is then carefully inserted into the belly. The excess fluid is extracted through the hollow needle. Doctors use ultrasound to show where the fluid is in the belly. If a large amount of fluid needs to be removed, the needle may be attached to a small tube that is connected to a bottle. The fluid then drains into the bottle. The procedure usually takes 20 to 30 minutes.

As you can see there are so many things that can happen while your waiting for a transplant. It's like playing dodgeball. You just got to keep ducking and dodging things as they come up.

The only use of an obstacle is to be overcome. All that an obstacle does with brave men and women are, not to frighten them, but to challenge them

- Woodrow Wilson

My greatest challenge while waiting for a liver was to remain within criteria and hope that the Cancer didn't spread outside of the liver or any of my lesions increase in size. To control the growth in my case they wanted to start me on chemo. I didn't have any idea what I was going to go through when I started this specialized chemo treatment. I only knew that people lose their hair and become extremely sick and tired all the time. It really didn't matter to me at that time because I just wanted to live.

They informed me that my chemo would be performed by an Interventional Radiologist instead of an Oncologist. The type of chemo procedure I was going to face was called Transarterial Catheter Emobilization (TACE) (*see terms*). The physician told me that Transarterial Chemo Embolization therapy involves administration of chemotherapy directly to the liver tumor via a catheter. With this technique, the chemotherapy targets the tumor while sparing me of many side effects of traditional chemotherapy that is given to the whole body. They placed me under a CT Scanner, so they could view the path of a catheter and direct it into the lesions in the liver. Chemo was then injected directly into the lesions. After injecting the chemo into the liver, they placed small beads into the arteries that fed blood and nutrients into the lesions, it will block the flow of blood and starve the lesions. The idea was not to treat the entire body with chemo and possibly damage other organs due to the toxicity of the chemo drug. Before you have the procedure done make sure you shave your groin area yourself the night before, so the nurses don't have to do it in the morning. You will probably be more comfortable shaving yourself than having to have a stranger handling your junk in that way. Before the procedure, they will give you a mild sedative, so you can be relaxed and reduce some of the pain and anxiety. The room will be cold so they will place two or three warm blankets on your body. In my case, they also played music that I liked to increase my level of comfortability. So basically you're laying there high, and they're playing some really good tunes. I didn't mind that part at all. They numbed the area in my groin area, so it wasn't that painful when inserting the catheter. This was the only part of the procedure that was slightly painful. Once you get past that part your essentially home free. I did feel some pressure during the procedure, but it's nothing that I couldn't tolerate. I needed to be awake so that I could take big deep breaths for them to see the catheter on the screen moving in my liver. The procedure doesn't take any longer than an hour. The prep time and the session will be about three to four hours. You will also have to be kept in recovery for at least another hour to be monitored before they move you to your room. Staying in the hospital one night was standard so they can make sure I wasn't bleeding from having to access my main artery. I would end up having 7 of these procedures done while I was waiting to get my transplant. I had so many procedures that they had to switch from my left side to the right side because the artery on the other side was just getting worn out. I never got sick after these TACE procedures, it just made me feel fatigued for a couple of weeks. The soreness in my groin area subsided after about a week. The entire process was done for one reason, and that was to try and keep the tumors from growing and keep me in the criteria. This treatment does not cure you of Cancer. It's just used to slow down the growth of the lesions or shrink them.

In addition to fighting the size and number of tumors, you may experience another very common symptom that is associated with liver failure. I've already mentioned ascites, jaundice, and thrombocytopenia, but there is one other one that you should know about. Another common symptom in patients whose livers are declining is called encephalopathy. Hepatic encephalopathy is a decline in brain function that occurs because the liver cannot adequately remove toxins from the blood. You may have difficulty with memory and focusing. You may also have trouble with problem-solving skills. Other people may notice symptoms in you before you do. A changing personality is one such symptom. For example, you may have been more outgoing than you were before the encephalopathy. You may have been much calmer than you were before the disease. You could also be lethargic and drowsy. I started to notice that my ability to concentrate was just not the same as it used to be a year ago. I was always able to sit down and work for several hours in the past, and I started to notice that I just didn't have the same abilities. My memory and attention span were severely diminished to the point that my family would have to remind me of things over and over. You may also have trouble with problem-solving skills and a change in your personality. There is no doubt this is one of the biggest and most dangerous issues for patient's families. Your family members must be more alert and definitely more patient with us. It's really hard to accept that you just weren't the same person. You become very defensive and sometimes can be abusive. Your ego is telling you that you're the same man and not wanting any help or sympathy, but truthfully your just unable to be trusted doing some things that not too long ago were very routine tasks. You start feeling less useful to the family and not as valuable. Roles in the house start changing, and your wife or caregiver starts assuming more and more duties. I can remember that several times I had started cooking and forgot that I had a pot on the stove.

Family members would have to watch me so I wouldn't hurt myself or others. It became a struggle for me because I knew that before having some of these symptoms I was a brilliant and a reliable person. It took me a bit of time to realize that I was still smart, but my body was just failing me. I had to accept the fact that I needed help. I had to make adjustments and never assume I was always correct. And that was hard for me because I enjoyed being right. LOL!! I started writing down everything and kept a checklist to ensure I didn't forget things that were important. People would ask me two or three times the same question. In the past, I would have been aggravated and assume they thought I was stupid. I got it in my head that I needed them and helping me was ok. This was the first time in my life that I knew I was not going to accomplish some tasks alone. I needed people in my life to carry me during these times because I wasn't going to be able to carry myself.

The doctors prescribed a drug called lactulose that helped with these symptoms. It's a really thick sweet liquid. It will have you going to the toilet quite often. I always said it gave me 'bubble guts". The drug is very effective, and it worked well eliminating most of the symptoms of the buildup of ammonia.

Just keep putting one foot in front of the other. You're moving forward, sometimes slowly and sometimes quickly.

– Eugene Brooks

I slowly moved up the list and continued to get those crucial points needed to get to a transplant. I knew I was getting close to that time to get the call from one of my nurse coordinators because my MELD score was around 32. I made sure I had my bag packed and in the trunk of my car. I didn't want to be in panic mode and forget anything I needed at the hospital. I didn't know exactly how I was going to react when I heard those magical words. During this period while waiting, I became an Amazon fanatic. I needed to do something while waiting for the call. Please don't go nuts, but it was a good distraction. So, I shopped online for stuff that I was going to need in my hospital bag. Make sure you have enough stuff packed for about a week in the hospital. I had plenty of underwear, pajamas, socks, sweatpants, flip-flops, toothbrush and paste, deodorant, an extra charging cable for your phone, and big t-shirts. Make sure to get some pajama tops that button up in the front. You will have so many lines connected to you when you get out of surgery that you won't be able to pull anything over your head. I kept all the things I would need in the trunk of my car so that I would be ready to go no matter where and when they called for the transplant. If you don't like hospital pillows and towels, then include those on your list. I always kept my phone with me and charged no matter where I went in case I was called. It's funny because before being put on the list I would never answer my phone when I didn't know the number. During that period I was answering every call. I didn't care if it was a bill collector, scam calls or somebody trying to sell some stuff that I wasn't going to buy. I was going to make sure that I wouldn't miss that call. Period.

    I mentioned earlier that I was staying with my ex-wife during this period because I needed to demonstrate that I had a support system. It was a requirement that you can show that you will have assistance before and after the transplant. As I mentioned earlier, it is crucial that you have people around you in case you start having symptoms from encephalopathy. My ex and I had a good working relationship. We had three boys, and we believed that it was important to show the boys that there was a certain type of harmony that existed. I thought it was an important factor in their development. Besides it being important for them it was equally important for me spiritually. I never liked conflict because the internal conflict can have an effect on you and your peacefulness. I also had a female friend, Kimyatta Sanders, who lived in Dallas that would routinely drive down to check on me. My ex's name was Kim and I would often call my friend by the same name. It gets stranger, just hold on. I swear I am not making this up to tell an interesting story. The two of them actually started to bond, and from this chance encounter, they became friends. Crazy right!! I can remember a couple of times all three of us would show up at the hospital for an appointment, and I would have to explain the situation to the nurses. They all thought it was different, maybe even weird, but would applaud us for getting along so well. I always believed that honesty in relationships was important. I am thankful that I always followed those principles because little did I know at that time it would aid me in saving my life. After repeating my situation with my ex-wife and ex-girlfriend, it started having me thinking about the kind of person I had been in the past. I also started to think more about the importance of friendship and love. The intangibles that we sometimes take for granted because we live in such a world where objects and money dominate our existence and thoughts. I will explain later in the book how all of these things played a role in my fight to live with Cancer.

You get into a routine with your normal doctor visits and scans while you are waiting on the list. It can be difficult waiting for someone to die so that you can live. I have been to quite a few group sessions with others who are on the transplant list, and they don't always connect with the idea that for them to live, someone must die. It was kind of sad that they didn't get it. It felt like they were disconnected from life, God, and having any compassion for another human being. It reminded me of myself twenty-five years ago when I was standing on a street corner on Biscayne Blvd. feeling totally hopeless. I was a homeless drug addict feeling disconnected from God, family, and if I'm honest just about everything. I was lonely and saddened about how I screwed up my life. I knew that God didn't love me during that time in my life. I knew that the abuse I suffered as a child was not my fault. It was God's fault. It wasn't until I got to treatment and became less ignorant about God that I was able to start connecting some dots. It took years to start understanding some of God's rhymes and reasons. It's never an accident that we go through what we go through in life. I sat in those group sessions praying that the other people in those sessions wouldn't have to feel the despair I felt that day in Miami when I was absolutely on empty. I had nothing inside of me but shame, guilt, and remorse that day in Miami. I know today that it is those things that keep us from the light. Of course, the people in my groups were not as depleted as I had been spiritually in the past, but they were as disconnected in much the same manner. I started to realize that maybe this Cancer thing that seems so terrible might be a blessing. I knew then just like I know now that everything happens for a reason. There were lessons here to be learned for me and everybody else in that room. Maybe the idea of someone dying for them to live was just too much for them to handle. Maybe they didn't feel deserving enough to accept such a huge blessing and would rather stay in denial about what was going to happen for them to live. It is a blessing, and frankly, none of us deserve to be blessed with such an awesome gift of life. Don't question WHY God has chosen you to live. It's purely by Grace. I would quite often ask myself, and the counselor at the drug rehab facility I attended when I first got sober thirty plus years ago why God would let me live and let so many people better then myself die. I had done so many things wrong in my life and knew I was not deserving of a second chance. He told me that we were not smart enough to try and figure out God's plan. The reasons for our blessings will be shown to us if we have our eyes wide open a clean vessel to accept them. For now, the only thing we can do is say thank you and follow the signs he gives to us as best we can. After that day I never felt unworthy of a blessing. I didn't deserve the blessing, but I was definitely worthy. I would just tell God – Thank You!! We must be humbled by the idea that God is willing to let one of his die for us to live. Take this new life and do something with the blessing if you make it to the finish and receive a new organ.

On the evening of May 25th, 2015, I got a call from Nurse Brown asking me if I was ready and how soon I could get to the hospital. I finally got the call that a liver was available for me. I told her I lived about 45 minutes away from the hospital and could leave immediately. My bag was packed, and I kept gas in the car, so I told her that I am on my way. She told me that I needed to report to the ER and I will be met by Dr. Cotton who will get me admitted and inform the staff to get me ready for the transplant. Keep in mind that there are at least 50 people at this point in the process who are working on making this surgery successful. The people at UNOS who distribute the livers are working to make sure the hospital who has the organ to be donated is informed that the liver will be going to a patient at the VA. A physician is heading to the hospital where the donor is being kept on life support to harvest the liver. The staff at the hospital where the donor is located is starting to get the operating room setup for extraction of the organs. Medical staff at the hospital that will be doing my transplantation are scheduling nurses, anesthesiologists, and blood product are being checked to make sure they have a sufficient amount of my blood type on hand. There are also people making sure the operating room is prepped and ready to go for the transplant, all the instruments must be sterilized and counted waiting in the operating room, the ICU room after surgery must be prepped and have all the additionals equipment needed, and pharmacists are getting medications that will be needed during and after the operation available for me. As you can see it's a very well-coordinated event that has to come together perfectly. There can't be any mistakes.

I jumped in my car and started driving to the hospital in total disbelief. The day had finally come, and I was going to make it. I had dodged death again. I had jumped through all the hoops and passed through all those obstacles to get to this point. I called some friends and family members letting them know that I was on the way to the hospital for my transplant. I also posted it on Facebook to inform other friends who have traveled with me on this journey over the last two years. You've waited so long and dreamed so many nights in anticipation about the day when you get the call. I was more excited than scared. The thought of not having a successful transplant didn't enter my mind. I knew that it was going to go well. I always kept in mind that I have been so blessed in the past and he surely was not going to get me to this point and not let me have a successful transplant.

I arrived at the VA and was quickly met by Dr. Cotton in the Emergency Room. The nurses in the ER started getting me prepped by getting my blood pressure taken, weighing me, checking my temperature and asking me all the normal questions that you have been asked at every appointment. Dr. Cotton got me checked in, and I was taken upstairs to my room to continue getting me prepped for surgery in the morning. When you're in the ER, you will have to change clothes and put on a gown before getting moved. They will ask you to give all your valuables to your caregiver who arrived at the ER with you before taking you away. I made a mistake and gave them my cell phone when I gave them the rest of my valuables. In my case, my caregiver was not allowed upstairs with me when I was getting prepped. You will see them again when they move you from the prep room to the holding area before your operation. You can give them your cell phone when you see them again. You will be in that room for a long time and will need it to keep yourself distracted and calm before your surgery. There was a gentleman I met in of our group sessions which was unable to have his transplant because he was so nervous that his blood pressure was elevated. The phone can be a great tool to keep you distracted. You might even want to get Netflix and watch some TV shows or a movie while waiting. Make sure to keep calm because it would be a shame to get this far and can't have the surgery because your blood pressure is elevated.

After I got upstairs, I turned on the TV and started watching a playoff basketball game. I remember that night just as if it happened yesterday. The Houston Rockets were playing in a Western Conference playoff game against the Golden State Warriors. The city was excited, and everyone in the hospital was fixated on the televisions cheering for our home team Rockets. I got my room organized and opened the curtains so I could look at downtown Houston from my bed. After being in the room for only a couple of minutes the nurses and staff members started their parade of visits. While all this was going on, I can remember it started raining. One of the physicians on duty came in and told me that my surgery had been scheduled for 6am. As time was passing, and people were coming and leaving it was still raining. No, it was pouring, and it wasn't letting up. The news channels were reporting about possible flooding here in Houston. Now I am hoping that the rain subsides long enough to get the organ and surgical team in here to perform the surgery before the organ is no longer usable. They have a 12-hour window from the time of extraction to the end of transplantation. So that time is ticking once they remove that liver from the donor's body. I'm not too stressed yet about the rain, but just a little concerned because if Houston gets two or three good drops of rain, it will start flooding.

About 2am the surgeon who extracted the organ from the donor arrived carrying my new liver in a Styrofoam cooler. Now that was strange seeing my new liver in a container that would normally house stuff like lunch or cold beer. The physician said he was very lucky to get to the hospital because it was starting to flood. He told me he tried a couple of different routes before he found a passable road to the hospital. As time passed, I started to get worried about whether the staff was going to be able to get to the hospital. Around 5 in the morning a doctor notified me that the surgery time had been pushed back three hours to give the team additional time to get to the hospital. I know that this just can't be happening. Really!! The night I get the call, and it starts to rain hard enough to flood. I was keeping a close eye on the news channel, and it was starting to look like that it wasn't going to happen. The news was reporting that at least nine inches of rain have fallen in the area around the hospital. A couple of hours later a nurse came to the room and told me that the surgery had been canceled. I tried to be optimistic about what happened over the last 12 hours, but I was extremely disappointed. I got dressed, cleaned up and was discharged about nine in the morning. I had to quickly turn my attention to finding a route to get home because I did not want to be stuck in the hospital. I was tired and didn't want to spend another minute at the hospital if I was not going to have the surgery.

   I was able to get home and was sitting at the edge of my bed thinking what the hell just happened. It seemed like a dream or some type of outer body experience. It took me a moment to get myself back on planet earth. I was so relieved when I got the call, and now here I was back in the same place I was yesterday morning. You talk about a roller-coaster ride. The highest of highs thinking that you were going to get saved and you will live through this Cancer nightmare, and a couple of hours later I was back to waiting. Back to hoping to get another call before something crazy happens and I get kicked off the list because the Cancer has spread. I immediately went back to my spiritual beliefs and concluded that it was a God thing and it just wasn't supposed to be. I mean what are the chances that we would get eleven inches of rain the night that I would get called to have my transplant. I didn't have anybody to blame. I did everything that I was supposed to do. All the planning worked just like I had dreamed about for the past two years. The doctors and staff at the hospital did what they were supposed to do. It just wasn't meant to be for me that night. They will tell you that there is a possibility that you get called and may get sent home because the organ that is being donated may be rejected by the surgeons after they do their exam. I knew it could happen, but it never crossed my mind when I got the call. All I could do was lay down and take a nap. I was emotionally exhausted. I was physically exhausted because I was up-all-night waiting in my room getting prepped for the surgery. It's a great example of not being in control. I pride myself on planning and executing that plan. All the planning in the world means nothing if God has a different plan for our lives. Control is just an illusion. We control nothing. It's important to plan and prepare so when a blessing does appear you will be ready for it. It must be balanced with the idea that if your will and God's will don't line up, then it just isn't going to happen. We must remain balanced and flexible.

Just four days later on May 29th, 2015 about 8pm Nurse Brown called me again. I knew exactly what I needed to do and where to go. I was still excited even though it was the second time. I followed my same steps as I did the first time. I contacted all the same people just as I did four days earlier when I got the first call. I knew for sure that it was going to happen, what are the chances right? Once I arrived at the hospital, the staff got me admitted and up to the third floor quickly. I knew that I needed to be prepped and go through a series of tests all over again. The most painful part of being prepped was getting the arterial line inserted in your arm. It was very different than just getting your normal IV started. They numb the area because the line is so much larger than a normal IV. This type of IV is most commonly used in intensive care medicine and anesthesia to monitor blood pressure directly and in real-time (rather than by intermittent and indirect measurement) and to obtain samples for arterial blood gas analysis. The nurse I had this time wasn't as skilled as the nurse who inserted the line the first time I got called for the transplant. She had to try multiple times before finally getting it inserted. I could tell immediately that my arm was going to be bruised because it started to swell pretty quickly. I was then moved upstairs into a little holding area across the hall from the operating room. I had gotten further in the process than the first time. I started to relax because I knew this time it was going to happen. A surgeon came to visit me and asked me a few questions and to mark the area where they would be performing the surgery. I couldn't figure out why they needed to draw lines on me where they were going to operate. I knew the surgeons were very skilled and in fact, the lead surgeon, Dr. Goss is considered to be one of the finest transplant surgeons in the country. Oh well, I didn't care I was just excited to finally get this thing over. The holding area was in an open area, and it was about 20 feet from the operating room door. All I needed to do was get put to sleep and wake up with a new lease on life. Minutes before getting pushed into the operating room I see Nurse Brown approaching me. I knew something wasn't quite right. She said that the surgery had been canceled because the surgeons didn't like the way the new liver looked. They said that it was fatty or something and didn't want to take a chance on transplanting that liver. Really!!! Oh God, not again. You just can't make this shit up. She said that she was sorry, but it was their call not to transplant. I asked her does the Doctor who removes the liver from the person donating it examine the liver to make sure that it's usable. Nurse Brown said that the physician does examine the liver, but it also must be reexamined again by the physicians who will be transplanting the organ. It's ultimately their call. I was just shocked!! This really couldn't be happening again. I knew that it could happen, but twice. And its things like this that make me have to write this book. This is the time for the short version of the serenity I mentioned earlier. Fuck it!! It is what it is. I was wheeled back downstairs to get all the lines out of my arms and sticky things off my body so I can go home again. A couple of hours later I was back at that same place as I was when they sent home the first time, sitting on the edge of my bed scratching my head trying to figure out what the hell just happened. There was nothing to do but take a nap and hope that God knew what he is doing. This kind of stuff only happens to me. Now I'm laughing with God. It's a good thing that this wasn't my first rodeo ride in life with God. There had already been so many peaks and valleys I've traveled that it didn't take me to far off center, but this was certainly testing my patience and belief. I just had to remain patient and keep moving forward. I was very disappointed but remained faithful that everything happens for a reason.

I didn't get depressed because I knew that it wouldn't be long before I get called again. It was just 4 days that I had to wait to be recalled the last time. A week had passed, and I really thought I would have been called by now. I started to learn more and more about how the waiting list can fluctuate. One day you can be at the top of the list, and the next day you can be fourth or fifth on the list. A patient's health could have gotten worse overnight that was behind me, and because of their decline, they get pushed ahead of me on the list because they have now become gravely ill. As much as I wanted to be transplanted, I couldn't be mad that I was getting pushed down the list. Somebody else needed worse than me.

I needed to keep moving forward with my program of patience, and it was now time for my normal 3-month scan. The following day after my CT-Scan I got a call from Nurse Brown with the results. She told me that I am now outside of criteria and I am no longer a candidate for a liver transplant. I just stopped what I was doing and sat down in shock. I couldn't believe it. She told me to come in tomorrow and see the doctors about how to move forward. One of my lesions was a centimeter too large, and according to the Milan criteria that I mentioned earlier I was no longer a viable candidate. I wish I could tell you that I was able to just let this news bounce off of me, but it was devastating.

It's OK to be mad at God, but you still must obey.

-Eugene Brooks

So, my God and I have a very honest and real relationship. He has saved me many times before and I have learned over time that it was OK to be mad. God and I had a very real conversation that day after I got off the phone with Nurse Brown. I told him that the shit he was doing was not funny. Yeah, I cussed at him. Listen, he knows that I use four-letter words occasionally and he isn't that thin-skinned. I told him he could have gone about this whole thing a lot differently if he wanted to teach me something. I had to tell him how I was feeling. Don't judge me, it was a rough day for me. In fact, the last three weeks have been a test of my patience and faith. I also told him that I will always obey and accept whatever he has planned for me, but today was not the day for him and me to talk. I knew that God could never do anything routine-like for me. The story of my life has never been normal. There have always been these twists and turns. There always must be this big magnificent story in my life. I didn't feel betrayed. I didn't feel he didn't love me. I just felt disbelief because I had been called twice and sent home. I told him that sometimes I don't know if I can handle everything that he expects from me. I was doubting myself and my own strength to shoulder his expectations. I wouldn't mind having a normal routine transplant like others have had in their life. I just don't have to be extra all the freakin time. I knew that God loved me and wanted the best for me based on all the miracles that have happened previously in my life. Who goes from being a homeless drug addict to graduating and getting a Bachelors Degree and then earning a Juris Doctorate Degree from Law School. There have been numerous amounts of miracles that he has performed for me. I just couldn't find an answer to that WHY question. I knew I needed to get myself together.

I had to start moving into the acceptance phase of what was going on. I had to remind myself that I had already lived longer then what I deserved. It was only by grace that I had survived this long and had experienced so many memorable moments. All the drugs, criminal behavior, being homeless and alcohol I consumed over 30 years ago were not recipes for a long, fruitful life. I also knew that I wasn't the same person as I used to be 30 plus years ago. I had been clean for over 30 years and have turned my life around. I also knew that as a child a bullet grazed my head and I was also electrocuted at the age of ten. I started thinking that I needed to be a little more grateful. Acceptance was a process, and I was going thru it. Anger and being pissed is always the first step which I accomplished beautifully. I had learned a long time ago not to take my anger out on people. They usually don't have anything to do with the problem. They become collateral damage, and after you calm down, you then must go back to them and make amends. If you're lucky, they will be there to accept your apology. If this destructive pattern of behavior has happened previously too many times, they just might not be there for you anymore. The sad part its usually family members who get most of the anger. We sometimes just like to take it out on somebody, so we don't have to deal with it or look at our own fears. Fear came over me and the thought of dying rushed into my mind. I needed to just sit my ass down and take a big deep breath. I had no one to blame for me not getting the two livers. I had nobody to blame for having contracted Hep C, which eventually leads to Cancer and me needing a transplant. All the nurses and doctors did everything they could do to get me transplanted. So, when all else fails, go ahead and be mad at God. I can't be that either since he has shown me so clearly with all the lifesaving miracles he has pulled off that he loves me. I knew I needed to sit down and exhale.

Acceptance is the key to life.

Resistance to that change is

what causes pain.

—Eugene Brooks

After a day or two of thinking about my past, I was able to find some peace about my situation. It was simply God's will. I came to accept the fact that some people's journeys are just different from others. God has given me an awesome responsibility, and I had to shoulder that responsibility. I was now at a place to exhibit the courage to change the things that I could. I had always thought of myself as a fighter and believed I had been taught enough by God to be able to stand up and walk through anything that God wants me to face. I knew it was time to get back to the action part of life and get my ass to start moving forward. I was still fearful, but it was not going to stop me from walking through that door of the unknown. I don't want you to think that I was some type of spiritual machine. I'm human, and I accepted all my human traits a long time ago. I am a spiritual being, having a human experience. Part of being a human is being fearful. I thought of an acronym that I was taught many years ago. FEAR False Expectations Appearing Real. I needed to remind myself that I was not living in the right now. I was getting way ahead of myself and letting fear drive my mind into all kinds of craziness. It was time to just slow down and get back to One Day At A time.

I've always been able to speak to Nurse Jones, and I knew that if I were going to get some straight answers, then that would be the person I had to call. All I wanted to know was the truth. I could handle whatever I was going to have to face. She said that they have had cases before that patients would fall outside of criteria and they were able to get them recertified and back on the list. That's all I needed to hear. All I needed was just a little bit of hope. I didn't always believe in what the doctors told me, but I could hold on to what Nurse Jones told me on the phone. I didn't have to question whether what she told me was a lie or the truth. I knew it was the truth and knew God had placed her in my life for a reason.

At the appointment, it was suggested that I go through additional TACE procedures to shrink the lesions so that I could be recertified for the transplant list. I really didn't feel a great deal of confidence from anybody on my medical team except for Brown and Jones. Looking back, I can say those feelings of a lack of confidence were fueled by fear. In moments of fear, I become extremely focused and patient while waiting for a sign on my next steps. The message always comes, we must be clear and focused on finding the messenger. Jones was my messenger. I respected all the physicians, but I had built a certain trust with Nurse Jones. This is the reason I mentioned earlier to find your person when starting this journey. That's all I ever needed in life was just a string of hope to hold. Yes, I was fearful, but not so fearful that it would change my attitude or compromise my happiness. I remained a glowing spirit wherever I went and continued to tell my story of the struggle I had faced in my life. I remained in faith and tried to comfort others and give them the same amount of hope that Nurse Jones gave me. Doing those things helped me regain my footing. Many of those moments of trying to give hope to others immediately after the news was all fake. I knew it was and I also knew that it didn't matter what I believed at that time. I remembered what I had been taught a long time ago. Fake it until you make it!! I was going to keep drinking my own Kool-Aid until I got the message that I was spreading. Yeah, sometimes you just got to hold on until the miracle happens. The best way to get out of your fear is to help another person. You would be surprised how much a little bit of hope can carry a Cancer patient. Maybe this was the reason God gave me this journey. We Cancer patients go through so much for such a long time that the will to live can be broken bit by bit. We start to get tired of doctor's appointments and living in fear. I was fortunate that I had young kids that kept me going and unwilling to give up. I have seen other people succumb to their fatigue and just want it to be over. It's remarkable how resilient you can become if you have a reason to live. As fast as medicine is evolving today, there might be an answer coming for your illness at any time. You just have to hold on because no one can tell what's going to happen in the future. Don't get me wrong the idea of dying from time to time would cross my mind. A friend of mine, Kimyatta Sanders who I mentioned earlier, told me that I was so fortunate. She said," You don't have to get ready; you're already ready." It took only 10 seconds for that statement to sink in. The idea of death is also something that we must accept. It's always been my desire to die with a clear, peaceful mind. I didn't want to lay in that bed with any "I wish I would haves." I have always tried to live my life for those last two minutes of my life, and I want to lay in that bed knowing I gave life a run for its money. I didn't want life, which includes Cancer, to beat me down.

A man is not finished when he's defeated; he's finished when he quits.

– Richard M. Nixon

A couple of weeks later I found myself once again laying on a table about to have another Tace procedure. I was all prepped and ready to do this again for the 7th time. The Doctor came into the room, and we exchanged the typical hellos, and then he asked if I was ready. What happened next sent me on another rollercoaster ride. The Doctor told me that he was going to do all he could do to extend my life and make me comfortable….WHAT!! Extend my life. I almost jumped up from that table and wanted to stop the procedure. I told him that this is not the reason that I am here to extend my life. I told him in a very assertive tone that I needed these tumors shrunk so I can get back on the list. He seemed a little startled when I said that to him. I started to wonder if I was on the same page as the doctors at the hospital. I knew that Nurse Jones wouldn't lie to me. I knew that her faith in God was as strong as my belief. I also knew that sometimes faith can be blinding. Sometimes it can be used to live in a state of denial. I now became very worried about what my chances were for getting back on the list.

He examined my scans and then told me that it would be dangerous to perform the procedure on all five lesions at one time. The doctor decided that he wanted to break the chemo treatments up into two sessions because he had so many areas to cover and didn't want to do more harm to my liver than was necessary. The procedure went as scheduled. Afterward, I was taken to a room to be observed overnight as normal. You know I got right on the phone and called Nurse Jones. She calmed me down and told me she would investigate what happened. The plan was for me to have the two treatments and then wait six to eight weeks before being rescanned. All that needed to happen was that one tumor needed to shrink by 1cm. I kept thinking about what the Dr said who was doing my TACE procedure. I knew that the physician was leaving the VA within the next couple of weeks and maybe he had mentally already checked out. I always had great confidence in the doctor performing my Tace procedures. I knew he was brilliant and dedicated to his profession. I concluded that he didn't really review my file as closely as he should have and didn't know what the plan was for the treatment. I just held on to the idea that things will be as things are supposed to be, and God was just building a testimony for me as he has always done my entire life. I totally gave up on what I thought was going to happen. I knew that I couldn't just stay in my head rethinking every minute detail. This journey has had so many twists and turns with no rest areas to pull over and catch your breath that I just needed to let go and let God.

"I am never alone, my Soul guides me, and my Guardian Angels protect me."

-Anonymous

Nurse Jones called and said that they wanted to rescan me before the next scheduled TACE procedure. The original plan was to have both procedures then get rescanned after waiting 6 to 8 weeks. She pushed the team to get it done. Maybe Nurse Jones just had a feeling that it would be Ok. Maybe God was telling her it was time to get him scanned because I got something for him right around the corner. I got over to the hospital and was scanned and started waiting all over again to hear from Jones with the results. The very next day Nurse Jones called me and told me that my scan results have changed, and they can now send my information off to UNOS to get me reinstated on the list. I asked her how all of this would affect my standing on the list. Would I lose all my points? Would I be placed at the bottom of the list again and the waiting period would start all over. She explained to me that my status and points will be the same as it was when I got deactivated. I can't explain how grateful and relieved I was to God and my angel Nurse Jones. There will be times that we just have to wait for God. You can try and knock down that door of opportunity as many times as you want, and it just won't happen until its time. Usually when you're killing yourself trying to force something to happen the best plan is to just sit down and wait for God to do some work for you.

This was the second time in my life that a Nurse went

beyond what was required of them to save my life. When I was homeless, and in a detox center in Miami a nurse conveniently lost my paper work so that I wouldn't have to go back on the streets. You were only allowed three days in the detox center to wait for an opening at a residential rehab center. My time had run out, and it was time for me to be put back on the streets while I wait for a bed to become available. The nurse knew what was going to happen if I was returned to the streets. The chances of me staying sober and clean when your homeless is virtually impossible. When a bed becomes available, the detox center will contact you and inform you to return so you could start treatment. How in the world are you going to contact a person who's on the streets and homeless? That nurse knew that there would be no way I was going to have a chance, so she told me to keep my mouth shut and go back to the dorms. She explained to me that I was special and felt like I had a good chance of leaving all this bad shit behind me if I was just given a chance at rehab. After a few hours in the dorm, she called my name to return to the main desk. With a huge smile, she informed me that a patient at a facility had just relapsed and a bed was now available. She went further and said that the facility I was going to was perfect for me. She said that there was a counselor there by the name of Ron Simpson who was excellent. I was on my way to the Bayhouse Residential Program to get treatment and begin a new life.

Nurse Jones pushed the doctors so that I would have an opportunity to get back on the list and to be transplanted. It's always up to the governing board to determine if you get back on the list, but at least I had been given a chance. It would have been easy for Jones to just do her job. Her actions reminded me of the nurse from Miami who saved my life and went far beyond her job description to save me. Maybe Nurse Jones heard God say," this son of mine requires a little more attention." The similarities in these two pivotal points in my life are striking. It's moment like these that reaffirm my belief that there is a power greater than myself that is moving everything in our lives. This would not be the last WOW moment on this journey. The level of commitment and care Nurse Jones has for her patients is due to her love of God and her belief that she is fulfilling her spiritual purpose.

"Now is no time to think of what you do not have. Think of what you can do with that there is."

- *Ernest Hemingway*

Once placed back on the list it was about 6 weeks before I got the call again that another liver was available. It was Saturday night, November 7th, 2015 at about 8 O'clock. I have no idea why I got all my calls around 8. I'm not sure if that is a schedule that is routinely used to get the patient in for an early morning transplant or what. My youngest son and I had just sat down to eat when I received the call for the third time. Nurse Brown who had called me for the last two attempts was once again the voice I heard when I answered the phone. She told me that there was a liver available, but the organ was considered a high-risk donation. I asked her what that means that it was high risk. She explained to me that the donation was from an inmate from the local prison. She explained that the organ was screened the same way that any other donation would be scrutinized, and it was deemed to be acceptable for donation. She went further and explained that it was considered a high-risk donation because it was coming from a prisoner and while normally the donation is completely anonymous in these cases some information is given out because of the donors' actions while he was living. I understood what Nurse Brown was saying to me, and I also understood that there are people who believe that when you receive an organ from someone that you take on their personality or at least parts of their personality.

I am not one of those people that believe that this transfer of personality traits happens, but I did understand the reasoning for the disclosure. After Nurse Brown informed me about the donor, I started laughing. I knew at that moment the transplant was going to happen. A complete calmness came over me, and I had to just laugh and shake my head. My little voice inside of me that God gives us all told me that this was the liver that was designed to carry me through the rest of my life. God's plan will be revealed when it's time. Brown asked me why I was laughing. I told her that I would rather have a liver from prison then one from a church house. It was only appropriate that God would give me this liver. Everything made sense to me at that moment. This was another one of those moments that the similarities of the events just makes you shake your head and laugh. Here it was that the liver I get comes from somebody just like me. Maybe the old me, but it was still me. It didn't come from a perfect person who lived a relatively normal life. I get a liver coming from someone who has struggled in life and has been a disappointment to himself and others at some point in his life. This person has been in trouble with the law and society has cast him aside. He was no longer thought of as a productive member of society, but more like a burden. I was one of those people, and it was perfect that someone like me who was a burden on society saved me. The similarities of it all just put a smile on my face. I stood in the kitchen shaking my head laughing with God. I knew he was laughing, and I was laughing right there with him. I just kept thinking he must really be having a good time watching the show he orchestrated.

I arrived at the hospital and went directly to the ER just the same as the other two times. I knew the drill and knew exactly what to expect. Since I knew the surgery wasn't going to be until the morning, I had to stop and get that Whataburger hamburger with fries. Shh, don't tell that part to your caregiver, and please don't let me be a bad example. LOL!! I remembered starving the last two times. At this point, I'm getting way too comfortable with this whole transplant process. Maybe even too comfortable. Nah!! The Nurse coordinator called ahead of my arrival to put the orders in the system for the surgery in the morning and alert them that I would be coming in for the transplant. They will draw blood and check all your vital signs and order all the pre-op testing. By this time, I knew the procedure better than some of the nurses and staff on duty. LOL, in fact on several occasions I had to explain to a couple of staff members what needed to happen next because they weren't sure what needed to be done. The nurses on the 3rd floor knew my name and joked around with me when I arrived on the floor.

Several nurses stopped by my room to wish me luck, again. The x-ray technician came in and took x-rays of my chest to make sure my lungs were clear. An IV was started so I could get fluids because you are not allowed to eat or drink anything before surgery. Little did they know I was full as a tick. The most painful part of the pre-op once again was getting an arterial line inserted.

A doctor came in around 4 in the morning and explained to me the procedure and instructed me that the surgery has been scheduled for 6:30 in the morning. He told me that around 5:30 someone would come to get me and take me to the holding area. I didn't have any reservations or doubts that everything was going to be OK. I did my research on the two surgeons and knew that they were some of the best in the country. Dr. Goss and Dr. Cotton had my complete confidence. I guess when you know that they are going to cut a massive hole in your body and remove the largest organ we probably need to have some confidence in their ability. The time had come for them to move me to the staging area outside of the operating room. I had been here before when Nurse Brown informed me that the operation had to be canceled and I kept telling myself that if I see one of my Nurse coordinators I was just going to start screaming. Another physician visited me to make marks on my abdomen where the surgeons will cut me during surgery. I found it strange that they need lines to follow to perform the operation, but who cares, I'm getting this damn thing done today. If they don't know where to cut me, I was going to be in deep shit. I just had to ask him why he was marking me before surgery. He explained that they have many safeguards in place to ensure that the proper surgery is being conducted on the correct patient. That made perfect sense to me. I think we have all heard stories of surgeries that were performed on the wrong person. I'm sure every hospital has protocols in place today to ensure that those errors don't occur.

The time had finally arrived. The hospital staff started moving my bed into the operating room. I tried my best to stay in the moment and absorb everything as it was happening. I didn't want to just go through this event and not appreciate the effort and miracle of it all. I went through so much to get to this point, and I really wanted to relish every second. The room was very bright just like you see in the movies. It was much smaller then what I expected. I thought the room would be much bigger. It was about the size of a master bedroom in some of the newer houses. I had to slide over from the bed to the operating table. I remember looking at the table noticing that it wasn't very wide. I almost thought that it wasn't going to be wide enough to support me. I was really kind of worried that I would roll off the table. I guess if you're under anesthesia you're not going to move at all. It's not like you were sleeping and going to toss or turn. Anyway, Dr. Cotton came into the room and asked my name and last four of my social security number. He also asked me to explain to everyone in the room the reason for the surgery. This was again another way to make sure the right person was getting the right surgery. I was surprised that they were playing music in the room. I watched a lot of Gray's Anatomy and knew it happened on television, but never during a real surgery. I remember them listening to 70's or early 80's music. A sweet funky sound. I wanted to comment on the music with one of my snarky comments, but before I could put in my request the anesthesia kicked in, and I was knocked out.

Self-sacrifice is the real miracle out of which all the reported miracles grow

-Ralph Waldo Emerson

You and your family have finally gotten to the point you have dreamed and prayed about for the last couple of years. Be grateful that you and your family are experiencing this moment of salvation, but remember while at the same time another family somewhere is experiencing grief and sadness. Even though my liver came from somebody that society had cast aside because they were a prisoner doesn't mean that I shouldn't feel grateful. He was still a human being who obviously was a kind person. We know that because he decided to donate his organs. He knew at the time he decided to sign those papers that one day he was going to be able to save someone. Maybe he was also trying to right some wrongs in his life. This might have been his moment to wash away some sorrows and which would give him the ability to die in peace. I do know that there is always a blessing for everybody in every interaction in life, whether they are big or small. I keep talking about the blessing and lessons that happens all the time. Even in death, there is a reason why things happen as they do. My prayer at that time was for the other family to see the miracle that had just occurred in their lives. When we really take the time to think about the miracle that had just happened, it can be breathtaking. Some human being you don't know gave up a part of themselves so you can live. WOW!!

"Happiness is not something ready-made. It comes from your own actions." - Dalai Lama

My ex-wife, who was my caregiver, was there when I was wheeled out of surgery. She told me I kept asking her "was it over," "was it over." She told me that I asked her the same question about 6 or 7 times. I guess deep in my mind I wanted to make sure that the transplant actually took place. I just wanted to make sure it wasn't a dream. I'm sure part of me really couldn't believe that this long-awaited blessing had come to fruition.

I started waking up about 4 or 5 hours after surgery. When you start coming out of the anesthesia, don't be alarmed when you see a lot of stuff hooked up to your body and stuff surrounding you're your bed. When you get put under there is just the arterial line, and another line in your arm and when you wake up the amount of tubes has tripled, and there must be at least three or four bags of stuff hanging from poles and several machines and monitors tracking different functions of your body. While you're in the operating room, they will also start another IV in your neck. One of the goals that I wanted to achieve was not to wake up with the tube in my mouth that helps your breathing during surgery. I did a lot of research before my surgery and discovered that after surgery a breathing tube may still be in place if there are some issues with your breathing. It looked uncomfortable, and it would have prevented me from talking. LOL!! I like to talk, and I knew I was going to want to ask questions about the surgery when I became conscious. They tell you very earlier in this process to try and stay in good shape. Try and get some exercise so the surgery and the recovery will go smoothly. This was one of the reasons why I pushed myself to jog, walk and lift weights while waiting for my transplant. I knew that it would help, and I was glad that in my case I was able to wake up and the tube wasn't in my throat. Do what exercising you can before surgery, even if it's just sex. It's also very good for your emotional well-being. No, seriously. Get it in!!

When you wake up, you will also be equipped with these leg cuffs. They reminded me of a blood pressure cuff expect bigger, I found out later there called an IPC device. While using an IPC device, your whole leg is enclosed in a cuff. The cuff fills with air and squeezes the leg, much like a blood pressure cuff. Then the cuff deflates and relaxes. The process then repeats over and over. The compression helps move blood through your veins towards your heart. IPC also promotes the natural release of substances in your body that help prevent clots. Between compressions, the cuffs of the device relax, and oxygen-rich blood continues to flow in the arteries of your leg. You will hardly notice the devices working. It doesn't feel like a blood pressure cuff, which at times can feel uncomfortable when it's squeezing the shit out of your arm. The amount of pressure is far less and is not uncomfortable.

After waking up, a technician will come to the room to do an ultrasound on your abdomen. They will do an ultrasound to rule out any internal bleeding. They want to ensure that the organ, in my case my liver, was doing fine and working correctly. Your still heavily sedated and under the influence of morphine so don't worry you won't feel any pain as they rub the ultrasound wand over the area that a few hours ago was cut open and being pulled on so they could extract the Cancer riddled organ and replace it with your new one. The remainder of the first day is pretty much a blur going in and out because of the drugs. I'm sure you can imagine the number of times that you're constantly visited by nurses and physicians. Whatever amount you come up with multiply it by three and that will give you some indication of the parade of medical staff coming into the room. They monitor you so closely because you will be in ICU.

I set many goals that I wanted to achieve before getting the surgery. I read an article I found on the net that there was a woman in England who had a liver transplant and was up walking around 28 hours after her transplant. My goal was to be up and walking around in the same amount of time if not quicker. I didn't beat her time, but I was really close. When my surgeon, Dr. Cotton came in to visit me the next morning, I asked him if I could get up and start walking.

He asked if I thought I was strong enough. He knew I was in good shape and told me that he wanted one more ultrasound, and then I could get up if everything looked good. It ended up that 30 hours after the surgery I had the IPC devices off my legs and was on my way for my first walk. The nurses thought I was crazy and had never seen anybody up so quickly. It was important to me that I get out of that bed and start moving around. I can remember my mother telling me, "A bed will kill you. You just have to keep moving to cheat death". I didn't want to just lay there and stay drugged again for another day. In my mind, it was time to start the recovery process. It was time to move beyond the surgery and Cancer and start my life all over again. I was given another chance, and I didn't want to wait to get started living. I can't remember exactly how many more times that day I got up to walk, but I know it was more than twice. They told me it was important to walk because you don't want any blood clots to form in your legs. The next day I was moved out of ICU and into a regular room. This regiment continued for another two days of walking, sleeping and being disturbed by the parade of nurses and interns. The only issue I was having was sleeping at night. I had so much gas trapped inside of me, and I just couldn't get comfortable. All my vitals looked good, and after a day or two, the pain had subsided enough for me to start cutting back on the morphine.

The doctor came in on Thursday morning and told me that I was doing well enough to go home. I knew that the longer I stayed in the hospital, the greater a risk I was at getting sick. My immune system was so suppressed because of the medication to prevent rejection that it was much easier for me to get sick the longer I stayed in the hospital. Before leaving I had several nurses stop by to instruct me on how to take my new meds, food restrictions, and wound care.

One of the most important things, when you have a transplant, is to stop the body from attacking your new organ. Your immune system must be turned down significantly so your new organ can live inside your body. Nurse Jones came in and went through all the medications with me. I was given a binder that included a list of all my medications and the times that I needed to take them. I would have never remembered all the schedules without the book. The folder also contained a chart that I had to complete that tracked all my vital signs while at home. I had to weigh myself daily, check my temperature twice a day, blood pressure in the morning and night, and blood sugar levels at least four times a day. The caregiver is significant when it comes to assisting you when you arrive back home. The name of the immune suppression drug given to me was Tacrolimus. There are some risks associated with taking immunosuppressants. There is a higher risk of some types of Cancer, because of your body's inability to fight off viruses is weakened. You must make sure you are as careful as possible when you leave the hospital. The other drug that you will have to take for a short period of time that can have significant side effects is your steroid. Steroids will elevate your blood pressure and increase your blood sugar. They will give you insulin to shoot when you first leave the hospital to help you manage your elevated blood sugars. If you are not a diabetic before the surgery, more than likely you will be taken off the drug once you are tapered off the steroids. There will be a chart that will tell you how much insulin to shoot before each meal. The amount of insulin you shoot will be based upon your sugar levels. You will be given a glucose monitor and strips that you will use to test your sugar levels. The chart will be included in your handout, and the nurse will help you read it and instructions on how to administer the insulin. If you're unable to inject yourself, then make sure your caregiver can do it for you. The most important thing to remember is that you must make sure to eat after taking the fast-acting insulin. If your blood sugar drops too low, it can kill you. So, make sure you will be eating within 30 minutes after taking your insulin. I was diabetic before the surgery, so I had years of managing my blood sugars, but I was never insulin dependent, so all of this was new for me. This always created a little tension with my transplant team. I was very set in my ways on how I wanted to manage my blood sugars. I had always been very successful at managing my diabetes, and I wasn't quite ready to give them control of this part of my care. I followed their recommendations initially and eventually started to change a few things to fit my body makeup. I wouldn't suggest doing it the way I did it unless you have been a diabetic before the surgery. It takes a great amount of discipline to be compliant, so accept help from your caregiver. The biggest thing to remember is to eat, eat, and then eat. The worst thing in the world is for your blood sugar to get low. Make sure you and your caregiver pay close attention to times that you are scheduled to take your meds. It's crucial that you take your meds as scheduled. Make sure to follow the table of how much insulin to administer. Did I tell you to eat? Make sure to eat.

By far the drug that had the most significant amount of side effects was the steroid that was prescribed after my transplant to help manage the rejection of my new organ. Steroids can make you restless, bloated, nauseous, acne, depression, headaches, puffy face, anxiety, insomnia, etc. It got me a little crazy for sure. My sleeping habits were terrible. They even had me see a psychologist because they thought I was losing it because of the steroids. LOL, after seeing the psychologist they realized I was just a little crazy already, and the steroids were not the reason for my behavior. I just had a type A personality. So just be careful, and if you or your caregiver see these huge mood swings, then please let your physician know of the side effects. Again, don't worry this will just be for a short period of time that you are on this drug. They will taper you off the steroids pretty quickly. This is a list of some of the drugs that I will be on for the rest of my life - Ursodiol, Prilosec, Tacrolimus, Magnesium Sulfate, and Carvedilol. I had high blood pressure and elevated cholesterol, so I also take in addition to the other drugs Lisinopril and a cholesterol medication. Yeah, I know I was messed up even before this transplant. LOL don't judge me. LOL. It seems like a lot of drugs and changes, but you get into the habit of taking the meds, and it's not that big of a deal. Remember, the most important thing is that you will be living. A few pills a day is not that big of a sacrifice. The timing of the drugs is paramount. The times you take these medications must be damn near perfect, especially the Tacrolimus. Get into a routine and follow it as close as possible.

There will also be changes to your diet that you will have to make. You definitely are going to have to make sure that all your meats are cooked well. No more rare or medium rare steaks. I miss a T-Bone steak that has a little pink in the middle. The reason for this is to make sure that all the bacteria in the food is killed because your immune system cannot kill all those foreign bodies as it was able to do before the transplant. No more grapefruit juice or over easy eggs. Not sure why but it was on the list, so I just eliminated it from my diet. They will give you a list of things not to eat. Of course, they will provide you with the standard speech on the four basic food groups -Blah, Blah, Blah. Just make sure you get enough food because your body really needs the calories, so it can heal. Its working overtime and its needs the nutrition. I did notice that while I was sick, I did lose muscle mass so make sure to get your proteins in so that you can gain back some of your muscle that you lost.

Caregiving is a gift of Love

– Melodee Claassen

My mother flew down from Idaho to help me with my aftercare when I got released from the hospital. She did a great job caring for me. You will be instructed that you cannot drive for a couple of months after your surgery so you will need someone to drive you to the hospital for your appointments with your team after being released. Initially, you will have to go to the hospital at least three times a week to give blood. They will monitor you very closely for the next couple of months after surgery. This can be a tough time for caregivers who have taken on the task to provide love, support, and taxi services. Also, they are monitoring your meds and documenting all your vital signs.

Please be as patient as you can be with your caregiver. This is all new stuff for everybody. Your sleeping patterns will be all over the place. The steroids will have you restless, and you may be feeling a bit uncomfortable. Don't forget that you just had major surgery. The largest organ in your body was removed and replaced with a foreign object. I was bloated and unable to sleep in a bed when I got home so for the first couple of weeks I slept in a lounge chair. Sometimes I wish I would have taken the pain pills to go to sleep, but I was scared and didn't want to get addicted to the morphine. There wasn't a lot of pain, so I never even filled the prescription and didn't think it was cool to take them just to go to sleep. I wasn't getting enough sleep and coupled with the very early runs to the hospital to have blood drawn it kept me exhausted. I had lived by myself for years and was very accustomed to caring for myself, so it took some adjustment on my part to have somebody help me around the house all the time. The plan was for my mother to cook my meals, laundry, go grocery shopping, and keep me on my meds. I was only able to last two days being in the house before I decided to go grocery shopping. Remember what my momma told me about that bed killing you. They gave me a walker when I left the hospital to help me stay mobile, so I packed the walker in the car and two days after being home my mother and I were walking the aisles at the local grocery store. I had to stop three or four times, but I was moving down those aisles getting some exercise. I have always pushed myself, and I don't know why I thought this was going to be any different. On the days that I needed to give blood, I had to arrive at the hospital before 8am because my Tacrolimus levels needed to be monitored. They will keep a close eye on the levels to make sure the drug is adjusted correctly. If the dosage is to low the body will start rejecting the organ, and if it is too high you may experience nausea, trembling, chills, abnormal dreams, itching, and quite a few other unpleasant side effects. So, it's crucial that they get this dosage correct. They will keep an eye on your levels for the rest of your life to ensure that organ is protected.

I think that this is probably a good time to talk about the caregivers and our responsibilities to them a bit further then what I have written about earlier. Please take a moment periodically to think about all the sacrifices that your caregivers have made for you during this two or three-year period of getting to this point in your battle. Once you get to this point after being transplanted, you should stop playing the patient or victim role. Self-pity has never been attractive. Start encouraging your caregiver to start living their life again. It's time to disconnect and cut the rope of dependency. Doctors and nurses will probably tell you differently. After a couple of months, you should be able to be self-sufficient. This may be difficult for them and you. Many caregivers could start to get dependent on their role as being so vital to your survival that it will be difficult for them to disconnect. It has given them purpose and validation while carrying for you. What I'm talking about again is their purpose in life and their lessons that God may be trying to teach them while on your journey. There is always a two-way street with multiple lanes in a lesson learning journey. It's a superhighway with multiple lanes on each side that has no speed limits. Lessons and purposes in life change often during a lifetime. It takes you from one journey to the next in a blink of an eye. 24 hours is an extremely long time. Don't get stuck on a trip when the journey has ended. If the plane has landed, just get off and catch the next flight. Every journey will have phases and ending points. This is the part of the journey that requires change.

Once one Miracle happens, another one is waiting around the corner.

– Eugene Brooks

You and your caregiver are no longer waiting for a miracle to happen. The miracle happened at that moment when someone died so that you can live. Take a moment and think about what just happened to you in your life. This will usually happen after you have been home a couple of days and you have started to get in your routine with your meds and journaling your vital signs. Think about how happy you are that you have been given this great gift. Think about how your family feels and how happy they are that you will be with them longer then what you would have been if you didn't have this transplant. Think about your kids and how they feel that daddy will be around to be at the graduation, wedding, see the grand kid's birth, or any other special family event. Now take the time to think about the sadness that the other family who donated their loved one's organ is feeling at the same time you're celebrating. That special person won't see another birthday for himself or any other loved ones' birthday. They won't see any graduations, babies being born, or family vacations. The only thing they will be attending is their own funeral. I know I have discussed this issue earlier in this conversation, but it's so important and can't be talked about enough. So, take a moment from time to time and think about this beautiful journey. Also, start thinking about what you want to say in that letter you will be writing to the family that has just lost someone so you could live. You won't have direct contact with the family of the donor but if you decide to write a letter, which is the only decent thing to do, your nurse coordinator will make sure it gets to UNOS, and they will forward it to that family. If you're lucky, you will get a response from that family. Reflect on the journey, be thankful, and then turn the page and start on the next adventure.

Whatever you do don't question why you have been given this second chance and some other person won't be so blessed. I know I am repeating myself again but it's a very important part of your emotional recovery. I have spoken to quite a few transplant patients who don't feel worthy of such a huge blessing. Keep in mind that we don't choose the path of the journey. We don't control much in our lives. If you got a transplant, then you accept it and keep moving. If you drank too much before the transplant, then don't after the transplant. It's always a good time to change. If you have done and said things during episodes while dealing with encephalopathy forgive yourself. I know it's difficult especially with young kids, but they will understand if you give them time to realize that daddy was just sick. The scar on your abdomen will heal in time and so will any of the scars in the family. Begin the journey of recovery for both you and your caregivers. It's your time to become the caregiver and the one being concerned about how they are doing. Start getting off your ass and help around the house or whatever you can do to help your loved ones. One of the remarkable things about transplants, especially liver transplants, you start seeing improvement immediately. Your skin color, the eyes become white again, you will start to have more energy, and your stamina will increase quickly. It will take a couple of months to get it all back, but at about the three-month mark, you will be physically capable of doing all that is required to be a productive individual again. Don't go crazy and start lifting heavy shit, but most daily activities you will be able to complete. There isn't much left you must do after your transplant but heal and get yourself ready to resume your life that has been put on hold for the last couple of years.

There is one other thing of importance that will have to be taken care of with your doctor. The liver that was taken out of your body is biopsied, and the results of that study will be discussed with you by your physician. This is usually not that big of a deal. They will discuss with you the extent of the Cancer and the location of those Cancer lesions with you. You really shouldn't worry about it, but just remember it's still good to get all the information that you can about your Cancer. In my case, it was very revealing. Again, God always has some twists and turns for me. As I stated earlier, it was thought I had 5 lesions at the time of transplantation.

Also, keep in mind that because of the number of lesions and the sizes of those lesions I was deactivated from the list and was forced to have an additional TACE procedure. The results of my biopsy revealed that I didn't have 5 lesions at all. I only had three. Yep, not five, but only three. I don't know what the hell the CT Scans were showing and who was reading those scans, but they were wrong. They weren't even close. I couldn't believe that because of that error I was taken off the list. Thank God that Nurse Jones pushed so hard for me or I may have never been reinstated on the list to receive a transplant. What I also find curious is that I had the additional Tace procedure and the doctor was shooting chemo in my liver in areas where there were no Cancer lesions. Remember he initially thought his job was just to keep me living and not to get me back on the list. When you have those Tace procedures, you are under a CT Scanner that gives the doctors an image of your liver so they can guide their catheters to the right area to inject the chemo. I didn't give it too much thought at that time, but afterwards, I realized I made a huge mistake. If you ever get deactivated from the list because they are telling you that you have fallen outside of criteria go, get another scan from a different location. It's just that important. We are talking life or death. Don't worry about hurting someone's feelings. It's your life.

Another bit of information that was discovered from the biopsy was that I also had another form of Cancer besides Hepatocellular Carcinoma. They found that one of the lesions was Cholangiocarcinoma. I was told that both Cancers were not on main arteries and the doctor felt like I had an excellent chance the Cancer wouldn't return. He felt my prognosis was good. He didn't give me any additional information about cholangiocarcinoma at that appointment. This would be the very first time I became aware of this form of Cancer. My doctor didn't seem to be concerned about the second form of Cancer, so I didn't give it a second thought. I left the appointment feeling optimistic and unconcerned about the findings of my biopsy.

Sometimes the rollercoaster ride starts, and you don't even know you've been seated.

– Eugene Brooks

My second journey with Cancer started, and I had no idea. It's challenging for me to write about this part of my story because of my admiration and respect I have for the physician that took care of me. I don't know why he didn't give me more information at the time I received my biopsy about cholangiocarcinoma. Bile Duct Cancer (cholangiocarcinoma) is a very rare and deadly Cancer. There are approximately 2,500 new cases of Bile Duct Cancer diagnosed each year in the United States or one case per 100,000 people. There is no cure for cholangiocarcinoma. I can't believe that he didn't know the dangers of this form of Cancer. All the literature says that Bile Duct Cancer tends to recur very quickly after transplantation. The recurrence rate for Hepatocellular Cancer is between 10% to 15%. The rate of recurrence with hepatocellular and cholangiocarcinoma present in the liver together is substantially higher. I have read several studies, and the data would suggest that the rate of recidivism is between 60% and 75% based on the size and location of the tumors. This type of Cancer is often discovered in the liver, and I am entirely sure he knew the prognosis of someone who is diagnosed with cholangiocarcinoma. Because of his expertise and knowledge, he certainly should have known that my prognosis was not the greatest. I feel like I should have been made aware of how highly likely the Cancer would return. I made a promise to myself and to God that I would write only the truth about my journey. As I sit here and write about what happened saddens me. I feel a bit of disappointment in the physician. I feel like a father whose son has disappointed him. There was a relationship that had developed between this doctor and me. He was much more to me than just my doctor. I want to be perfectly clear about my feelings and thoughts about this physician. Nurse Jones would often tell me that the doctor asked her when we were going to get Mr. Brooks a liver, which shows a level of concern and interest in me. If I had to have another surgery, there is no one else I would rather have standing over me with a knife in his hand then that man. It's important to share this lesson no matter how difficult it is for me. I made a mistake and didn't do my research on my own about this Cancer. This is one of those big lessons from this book that should be remembered. Trust but verify. Do as much investigating as you can about your illness. I broke one of my own rules by not paying closer attention and not investigating what he said. I'm not sure about what could have been done at that time to treat this Cancer before it "presented," but the idea of not doing anything, or at least not knowing, is hard to accept. It's even harder to accept that the doctor couldn't provide me with an accurate prognosis. Yes, I do know that any physician can't always be 100 percent correct all the time. The indicators in my case were just overwhelming that the Cancer would return. I am pretty sure that he knew of this type of Cancer and its danger to me. I'm now going to approach this issue from a totally different angle. I also looked at this situation from a spiritual angle so that I can get a greater understanding. I do accept the fact God was in control and obviously didn't want me to learn too much, too soon. I may have *wanted* to know, but the truth is I didn't need to know at that time. I do believe that a doctor should always give you full disclosure about your prognosis. I can't say what was going on in the doctor's life that morning when he gave me the results of the explant. That's not my job. I do know that it was a God moment. I am grateful that the cholangio was not discovered before my transplant. If it had been discovered before my transplant, I would not have been a viable candidate for transplant. So, for that I am grateful. Secondly, you will see later in the book how and why I am framing it as another God moment. I chalk it up to a God thing. Both he and I made a mistake with this information. I should have done my research and followed up. My intentions for telling this lesson is simply to inform others that we should, "Trust, but verify." We need to always remember that physicians are humans. They have good and bad days just like we mortals. I know it's easy to forget that they may have a child at home sick or just came to work after an argument with their spouse, or may have other life shit that their dealing just like we do. We MUST be their keeper. I'm sure doctors won't like that line, but oh well!!. What I'm saying is that collectively we should do some research and help them with doing their job. Also, keep in mind that more and more we may have physicians from other countries that come from different cultures. They may communicate things to us in a different manner then what we are used to here in America. Based on my experience It can feel harsh and very abrasive. They don't mean any disrespect at all. You have to establish a relationship with that doctor so both of you are on the same page. It may be frustrating because it may make you feel like the physician is talking down to you instead of talking with you. It's crucial to establish lines of communication with your physician, so there is harmony between both parties. This Cancer journey is already difficult enough and you don't need another pain in your ass stressor to make it more difficult. So, try and work it out!

> *"How far that little candle throws his beams! So, shines a good deed in a weary world."*
>
> – William Shakespeare

At this point in my recovery, my liver was functioning beautifully, and most of my other blood results were good. My platelet levels never rebounded to normal, but there was no need for me to be overly concerned. I had a condition before my transplant called thrombocytopenia. Thrombocytopenia is a condition in which you have a low blood platelet count. Platelets (thrombocytes) are colorless blood cells that help blood clot. Platelets stop bleeding by clumping and forming plugs in blood vessel injuries. When you cut yourself, the platelets stop the bleeding, so you don't bleed to death. In rare cases, the number of platelets may be so low that dangerous internal bleeding occurs. My platelet counts were hovering between 90 – 100. A typical range is between 150 to 450. My numbers weren't great but nothing to lose sleep about either. It was good to have had a break from the worrying and living in anticipation of the next shoe to drop. I had a new lease on life, and the small things just didn't matter.

My life was moving forward, and I was getting back to functioning as a productive member of society. I was about six months post-transplant and was still being monitored closely by the transplant team. The time had arrived again for my normal three-month CT-Scan to examine the liver and other organs. As usual, you get the scan done and would normally have to wait a couple of days. When I got my results, the CT Scan revealed that there was a lesion in my lymph node in my upper abdomen area. WOW!! Here we go again. The hepatologist who had been with me through the entire process told me the best-case scenario is that it was Hepatocellular Carcinoma returning and not Cholangiocarcinoma. He needed to do further testing to determine the exact type of Cancer that was seen in the CT-Scan. I still wasn't connecting the dots. Remember, at this time I didn't have all the information about cholangiocarcinoma. I was still in the dark about this form of Cancer. This was only the second time I had heard of this type of Cancer. I still didn't understand why he thought one was worse than the other. While fighting Cancer those moments of the appearance of success you should relish. Hold on to them as long as possible because we know our reality can change with one lousy scan and we will once again be confronted with new hurdles or detours that changes our moments of relief. Part of me just wanted to stay in the dark about this type of Cancer.

My reality became perfectly clear in June 2016. The following day after having the additional testing done I got my results. What one doctor didn't want to tell me six months ago about cholangiocarcinoma was now being said to me by another physician six months later. My doctor called me and asked me if I had time to talk.

He then asked me if I was driving. He asked that I pull over and stop the car so he could speak to me. At this point, I knew that this wasn't going to be a good conversation. He said that he was sorry, and the results of the test showed that the lesion on my lymph node was cholangiocarcinoma. He told me that my prognosis was about 6 to 8 months to live. My head just fell, and I just tried to keep it together until I got off the phone with him. I immediately thought about my kids. During this time in my life, I had my three boys living with me. They moved in with me after the transplant when it seemed that I was going to be ok. I had two in high school and one in middle school. As I thought about my kids, I just started crying. How was I going to tell them this news? I had so much racing through my mind. My friend Mike met in the parking lot to talk to me. It was by coincidence that he was so close. What am I saying, it wasn't by chance, it was clearly a God thing. Mike had been a friend of mine for the past twenty years. He was one of a handful of people that really knew me. He has witnessed first-hand other obstacles that I have had to hurdle in life before. There was absolutely nothing that I couldn't share with him. He knew what I needed to hear at that time. He also knew that sometimes all I needed was somebody to just listen. I just had to cry. He didn't say a word and let me just get it out. He knew that I needed to just break down for a minute and have a human moment. He remained very calm while I was crying and mumbling about what I was going to do with the kids. Before I left, he told me that it was going to be OK and he wasn't worried about me at all. I had to get myself together before going home to face my kids. I still needed to continue with my day despite just being told that I had been given an expiration date of six to eight months. The kids still needed to be picked up from school, dinner still needed to get cooked, laundry folded, and I probably had to fuss at one of them about something. Teenage boys need guidance daily. Life just keeps going on despite what's going on in your world, and we must continue to meet our obligations despite our issues. It had always been them first, me second. I don't care if I get bad news I always must protect them.

 I didn't even get pissed at God like I did when I got kicked off the transplant list. All I could do was shake my head and eventually started to laugh as I got closer to the house. I had spent enough time and energy being sad and in shock. I got my 5 minutes to break down out of the way. I called my sister in Florida and shared what had been told to me by the doctor. She was my other rock and was always optimistic. She knew my complete story and refused to believe that it was my time to die. I knew I needed to move from the victim role into the fighter mode. My fight was not over. There was an internal war going on between the spiritual side and my human side. Spiritually I could tell that God has always been there for me. Based on my past experiences with God he has performed miracles in my life, but this was going to require a grand effort on his part. I would often tell people that I was God's favorite and sat as close to him as anyone. I would always say that jokingly, but deep down I meant every word. I have learned from the past that the best thing to do is always follow that little voice that lives inside of us all. God lies inside of our hearts, and the devil exists between the right ear and the left ear. We can think ourselves into confusion and depression, and I didn't want to add any more drama or chaos to this situation. I thought of all these things as I was driving home. My human side was telling me that there is an end to all of us, and at some time in our lives, we must be adults and just accept our end. It would have been easy to just accept what my human side was telling me. If I accepted that thought, I wouldn't have to fight anymore. The truth was that I was tired of fighting. I had been through so much for so long dealing with this f**cking Cancer. I just wanted it to be over. My spiritual side kept telling me that you are about to see the greatest love that God can show you. My human side was telling me that you had a good run and sooner or later everybody gets hit playing dodgeball. I mentioned earlier in the book that God takes me through things for a reason. I just don't do normal shit. There always has to be this dramatic show. Deep down I just felt that I would experience a miracle and that everything was going to be ok. I knew that I was not deserving of a miracle, but I did know that I was worthy. There is a distinction between those two things. I had already been given more then I deserved in life. I also knew that I had helped others with male childhood sexual abuse, drug addicts, and alcoholics who were trying to get clean and sober. Because I had so much work helping others I felt worthy if God were to perform a miracle. The battle lines were drawn between my human side and my spiritual side. My human nature struck the first blow and wobbled me, but it didn't knock me out. The little light that I have always thrown to others had not been extinguished yet. It doesn't help and damn sure isn't productive being in the sad, poor me phase. I needed to get information about this Cancer and start to develop a plan. My immediate attention needed to be placed on me keeping up a façade so my kids wouldn't be traumatized.

After an hour or so thinking about the diagnosis I just accepted that this is God's plan for me. I couldn't understand why and I knew that I was incapable of knowing God's will all at one time. Like it or not, this is God's plan, and I was going to ride this thing out with a smile on my face. I have always followed my inside voice in the past, and it has never failed me. For the past thirty years when there was a tough decision to be made I always followed my inside voice. I always promised myself that when I leave this world, it was going to be standing on my feet and not laying down. I became more determined to not let this Cancer thing distract me from my primary purpose in life – HAPPINESS!!

If I knew anything after all that I had been through in life was that I had a purpose. God has always been there for me and protected me. That doesn't mean that I would never experience moments of discomfort and doubt. I thought about the bullet that grazed my head, the past sexual abuse, self-identity issues, drug addiction, homelessness, incarceration, and all the problems surrounding my liver transplant. Keep in mind that before all the issues with my health I had already published a book that dealt with my past and how I have always been shielded by grace. There was Hope for me. Let me share a secret with you. There is always hope for you and your loved ones too. Cast your light on the world. We're not obligated to save the world, just to help a few along our way.

The voyage of discovery is not in seeking new landscapes but in having new eyes.
- Marcel Proust

I accept that God has given me a gift to see what others are unable to see. He has always sent me a message. That message comes from the most unlikely of places. Isn't that where they always come from? Mine have. I have gotten my best messages from people who don't have the amount of formal education that I have, money I've earned, or status in society I have been able to obtain. I just needed to keep my eyes open wider than ever before if I was going to see his messages. I knew I needed to be carried on those days that my human side was winning the battle. Ironically enough homeless people have given me some of the most eye-opening messages. And look, I even got a liver from a convicted felon, an undesirable. I just needed help and direction. I needed to stay positive, and around positive people, so I could channel their energy. I had to stay away from negative energy so I could continue to be cleared eyes to see the messages that God would be sending me. I also knew that I wasn't going to do this alone. I needed to reach out to people that God had placed in my life, both past and present. I needed to build an army for this war. I needed like-minded people who saw the end game just as I had pictured it in my mind. I needed emotional support and medical advice to form a plan of attack.

I started to research this form of Cancer that the physician said would kill me. I read all I could that night, and none of the findings discredited what the physician told me. I could only find one case were a woman survived cholangiocarcinoma. It gave me some hope, but I still couldn't entirely shake this sinking feeling that my luck or blessings were coming to an end. My outlook on life and all my spiritual knowledge was keeping me from sinking further. I had to get back to the basics of living life. It's always been living my life one day at a time. It sounds so cliché'ish, right? The truth is that it has always worked for me. It's all I knew, and it had never failed me. I thought about all the lessons that God and life had taught me since I was saved from being a homeless drug addict 32 years ago.

The secret to change is to focus all of your energy, not on fighting the old, but on building the new.

-Socrates

Twenty-four hours is a long time, and life takes many twists and turns in a single day. The morning that I got that call from the doctor, everything was going smoothly. I felt fine and was making plans for my future and the future of my kids. In just a few hours my life changed, and I was heading in a totally different direction. Just remember things change very quickly in this cat and mouse game with Cancer. I became determined to not let this new information attack my spirit. I made peace with the idea that I could die, and still had the fight to keep pushing forward. I had to take into consideration the idea that it might be God's will that I die. I can't predict the future, and I certainly couldn't figure out why God does what he does, and when he chooses to do them. I learned that the resistance of God's will is what creates pain. The resistance to what is happening in our lives creates more pain for us than the actual occurrences in our lives. My only wish at that time was to be able to live long enough to get all my kids in college. I knew that while I was living that I had to do all that I was supposed to do for them. That was my responsibility/job that God had entrusted to me. All that I have, I must share with them. The most important of those things is my experiences in life and my relationship with God. I had to share the lessons that I had learned. I believed that then, and I still believe that today.

It's vital that we accept our lot in life, but it doesn't mean that we stop fighting for our lives. I knew that I wanted to be treated somewhere different than the VA for my Cancer. Based upon what that doctor at the VA told me I figured that there may not be much that they could do for me. I just didn't feel comfortable putting my life in their hands after all that I had discovered. If the doctor has no hope for your survival, then it might be time that you move on to another facility. The doctor may have wanted the best for me, but if he came to that prognosis, then he had lost faith in his capabilities, and the capabilities of the institution that he works with, to save my life. If he believes that he can't do anything, then he can't, and it's time to go.

I had several old girlfriends that were in the medical profession, so I immediately reached out to them. I had always stayed in contact with them while I was going through the process of getting a new liver. Thank God that I ended all my relationships on a positive note. I never cheated on women that I dated, and I always treated them with honesty and respect. You never know why people come into your life and you should always protect those relationships and not take them for granted. If my relationships were going to come to an end, then I wanted me and that person to remain friends. Earlier in the book, I mentioned that my ex-wife was my caregiver during the transplant process.

Our marriage ended, but our friendship continued. It was good for the kids, but it was also good for my spirit. Of course, there will be some people who think that it's just not possible, but for the most part, all my ex's and I were and still today friends. The two women that I contacted for help worked for MD Anderson Cancer Center here in Houston. One of them was a nurse and worked in the oncology department, and the other was a patient advocate at the hospital. I contacted the nurse first and told her what the doctor said, and she immediately started on working on getting me into MD Anderson to see the physician who worked in her department. We all know that the faster you begin treating Cancer, the better your odds are at controlling or at least slowing down the growth of the tumors. She contacted me the next day and instructed me that I needed to get all my records over to the physician that she worked with, so my files can be reviewed. She also got me scheduled to see the doctor in less the two weeks. Now that's a miracle to get in that fast especially at the world's finest Cancer hospital. It gave me some relief that I was doing all that I could possibly do to beat this Cancer. I was able to get my records to her very quickly because I frequently downloaded all my records and kept them in a file on my computer. I had all my records included blood results, any procedures, CT Scans, and doctors' notes, and within an hour they had everything.

If there is one thing you should take away from this book, please keep track of your records. You never know when you will need them. You don't want to try and get everything together if there was an emergency. I would frequently login to my account at the VA hospital and download my records. I also printed all my documents and created a binder so I could take them with me on every visit when I was on the transplant list. If you don't keep all your records in your binder, please keep at least a list of all your meds with you. Even today I have a list in my glove compartment with my insurance card in case I get into an accident so that medical professionals will have some idea about my medical history. Once a doctor looks at my list of prescriptions, they will be able to tell that I have high blood pressure, diabetic and have had a transplant.

Because I had everything organized on my computer I was able to email the doctors at MD Anderson that evening. People travel from all parts of the world to be treated at MD Anderson, and I was only a thirty-minute drive away. I always believed that I was solely responsible for my actions, and not the results. I accomplished what I could that day. I made contact with good people that wanted to see me succeed and followed through with all their instructions. It had been a good productive day. I was back to one day at a time.

That's all I could handle to keep from losing the battle. I was totally helpless again very much like I was when I was waiting for my transplant. I just had to keep living my life. I had to keep raising my kids and try my best not to let my fight with Cancer take a toll on them during this stage of their lives. I knew at some point I was going to have to inform the kids that the Cancer had returned, but just not that day. I didn't have enough information yet about this form of Cancer to explain to them what was in store for their father. I had never been big into creating drama and pity, so I didn't see the good in telling them yet with such a limited amount of information. I knew that the day would come, and I would need to have that difficult conversation. I just needed to keep on my path and keep doing what I had always been doing. Things always worked out exactly as they were supposed to be for me. I liked what I was getting so I decided to keep doing what I had always been doing in the past.

Simplicity, patience, compassion. These three are your greatest treasures.

– Lao Tzu

Time couldn't go fast enough as I waited to see the doctor at MD Anderson. While I was waiting for my appointment, I researched the doctor I would see at my appointment. Her name was Dr. Rachna Shroff, and one of her specialties was cholangiocarcinoma. I looked into some of her writings that she had published and to see if she was involved with any clinical trials. I knew that the trend for combatting some forms of Cancers was immunotherapy (*see terms*), but I wasn't sure for if they were attempting to use that therapy on patients like myself. Normally your immune system is alerted when there is something in your body that is not supposed to be present. That can be viruses, bad cells, or foreign objects, like a new organ. Your body doesn't recognize Cancer cells, and that is the reason it doesn't try to attack and kill those cells. The reason they are not recognized as an enemy to your body is that the Cancer cells at one time were healthy and have over time changed into cells that are killing you. It's like getting married to the love of your life and as time passes they change and have now become a pain in your ass. LOL, well kinda like that. Just joking. Since the original cells were seen as a part of your body even though they have changed your body doesn't recognize them as being a problem. They are wearing a mask, and it looks as if they are still good for you. Immunotherapy takes the mask off the cells so your body can see them for what they really are – a killer trying to harm you. They are having great success with this treatment for some forms of Cancer and more research is being done in all areas to combat Cancer.

I wanted to become confident in Dr. Shroff's level of expertise in this area of medicine. I had always researched the bio's of all the doctors I had seen while on this Cancer journey, but the stakes this time were much higher. Hell, I was just given a death sentence, so I needed to have some confidence in this doctor's abilities and interests. After reading everything about her, I became comfortable and confident. This was the doctor I was supposed to have to walk me through this next phase. I think about it now, and it was quite remarkable that I was so calm at this point. I couldn't fight what was going to happen to me. I always like to think about what happens to me in life as waves in the ocean. The water is always moving in the ocean. Our lives are always moving and changing. There is no way you can fight or change the movements of the ocean. You just can't do it. The ocean is much too large and powerful. Life is much too large and powerful. Since you can't stop the constant motion or change its direction, you only have one option; ride the wave. Go with the direction of the movement and try to ride that joker to the shore. Once there, then just breath, exhale and live.

I made it to my appointment and after waiting about an hour was taken back to see the doctor in a small examination room. We have all sat in those rooms waiting anxiously for the doctor to come in and deliver either a bit of hope or a clearer path to our death. As much as you don't want to be nervous, your nervous as hell. You can try and control your emotions, but that little room can drive you nuts especially if you're alone. You're just hoping that the doctor will hurry the hell up and see you as soon as possible. Dr. Shroff made it to the room and was very business-like. She was maybe even stoic, and I couldn't get a good feel for what she was thinking. She asked me all the normal questions you usually get when visiting a doctor, especially for the first time. She asked me about my transplant, meds I was taking, and my family history. She told me that the tumor was inoperable because it was in the lymph node right above the liver. I asked her about how successful she had been in the past treating cholangiocarcinoma. She said that she has had some success. That's it. I was hoping she would have expanded a bit more on her answer, but I got nothing. I wanted to ask her to go into further detail, but I was scared to ask because I might get an answer that I didn't want to hear. One thing I have learned through my entire time-fighting Cancer is that physicians who care for Cancer must have a different approach feeding their patients information than most other doctors. I first thought that Dr. Schroff should have given me much more information then what she offered at my first visit. It's hard for them to give too much information because Cancer is different for each person. The type of Cancer may be the same, but the patient's genetic makeup is different for each person. How that patient and their Cancer will react to treatment cannot be concretely predicted. There is a science to it, but it's not predictable with any degree of certainty. Today I understand her answer. I thought at that time she was trying to keep me from being hopeless and wanted me to keep fighting. Maybe that was the case, but it's also true that she just wasn't sure what was going to happen. As long as Dr. Schroff didn't say that there was nothing that could be done I was going to take that answer non-answer and run with it. It was a lot better than I was going to die in six to eight months. Remember all we want is just a little bit of hope. I didn't want to know more because it might taint the little bit of good information I just received. She did say that because it was such a rare form of Cancer that the medical industry has progressed slowly on a treatment. She wanted to start me on a combination of chemo drugs called Gemcitabine (Gemzar®) and Oxaliplatin (Eloxatin®). This combination of drugs was the standard protocol for treating cholangiocarcinoma. She explained that chemo drugs attack cells that are dividing quickly, which is why they work against Cancer cells. But other cells in the body, such as those in the bone marrow (where new blood cells are made), the lining of the mouth, intestines, and the hair follicles, also divide quickly. These cells can also be affected by chemo, which can lead to side effects. She prescribed me some medication to help me with nausea and other side effects of chemo. The chemo treatments I had when I was waiting for my transplant were totally different from this conventional form of chemotherapy (*see terms*). The side effects of traditional chemo were going to be much tougher. I didn't know what to expect when I started chemotherapy other than the horror stories and seeing patients walking around the hospital bald, skin color that was chalky, and looking extremely fragile. I knew that there was going to be a chance I would lose my hair, experience a lot of nausea, fatigue and just look sick. I figured it was time that I tell my kids about what was going to happen because I knew that I couldn't keep it from them any longer. I was pretty sure that I was going to need them at some point.

I finally made it to my car in the parking garage and just sat there for a few moments to breath and digest my morning. I knew that I had cancer, but it became so real after my appointment with Dr. Schroff. I am now a patient at MD Anderson, the world's best Cancer hospital in the world. When I walked into the hospital, I couldn't believe how many people were there fighting Cancer. Intellectually I knew that there are millions of people who have Cancer but to see it with my own eyes was shocking. When I went to other hospitals, you would have to guess why that patient was there and what ailment was being treated. At MD Anderson you didn't have to try and figure it out. Every patient there was being treated for the same thing ….. Cancer.

There is a Quiet and Hidden Beauty in Cancer

-Eugene Brooks

One of the benefits of having Cancer is the opportunity to heal some past wounds and become closer to some people in our lives. Unlike some other ailments or accidents, you don't die immediately from Cancer. Your given some time to get your affairs in order. In fact, you might be able to find some things that have evaded you your entire life. You just might find love, forgiveness, and a bit of peace of mind before you move on after Cancer. Words that you wanted to pass your lips can flow like water now because there is a chance of you dying. In my case, Cancer gave me an opportunity to know and love a sister that I knew of but never had much interaction with most of my life. My father had two kids before he married my mother. We knew of each other but just didn't connect. After being diagnosed the first time with liver Cancer, I reached out to my sister Regina, who lived in Florida, to try and open a dialogue so that I could get to know her a little bit better. I didn't have the same opportunity with my brother Michael because he had passed away several years earlier. What ended up happening I could have never dreamed would occur. She and I were pretty much identical. She was definitely a Brooks and was definitely my father's daughter. We talked probably four or five times a week. I kept her informed step by step through the entire transplant process. She ended up being my other go-to person when I had bad days. People usually love their relatives just because their your relatives, but I found myself loving her because of the person I discovered during this supposedly dark time, and not just because we were connected by blood. My journey with Cancer gave me a sister. I knew that this was a chance to grow and teach with my boys in the same way I did with my sister. I tried to always remember that the blessing or miracle we receive is always for everyone. I hoped that both my children and I would learn from this experience. I didn't fully know why God had put me in this position, but I knew it was for a reason and I wanted to take advantage of this seemingly horrible situation and turn it into something good. I wanted to teach them the lessons that God had shown me. I may not have known what the lessons were, but I had enough faith to know that whatever I said was going to be things that were meant to be said. Things that they said were just as important for me to grow. Cancer just couldn't have been just for me. Cancer was going to give my boys and me something for all these years that we have spent fighting cancer.

    I decided to tell my two oldest boys, ages 18 and 16, that the Cancer had returned, and I would have to undergo chemotherapy. I expressed to them that I may need their help around the house because the type of chemo I would be receiving will be different than the chemo procedures I received for my liver in the past. I painted an optimistic picture of what was going to happen and the results that I hoped to achieve. We all agreed that my youngest didn't need to know yet. He was only 12 at that time, and we didn't want him to worry. It was important to me that it was a family decision. I wanted them to feel that they were playing an active role in the process. We have always had an agreement that we would be truthful with each other no matter what. It was important to me that I build this foundation of trust with them so if they needed to disclose something to me they would feel comfortable doing so. I always preached to them about being a man. Forgive me when I say a man, but I was raising men. I wanted them to act like men and learn that you don't give up just because it gets hard. I always believed that it's more important to show your kids how to behave then just tell them how to conduct themselves. I wanted them to see that in difficult times you keep your head down and keep moving forward. Being a man/woman in this life requires for you at times to grit your teeth and go through things that are uncomfortable at times. You will have to walk through those doors of fear and uncertainty during a lifetime. I wanted them to see that you walk through those doors standing on your feet instead of God having to drag your ass through those doors kicking and screaming.

You're going to have to go through those doors of life, but you have a choice how you are going to do it. It's guaranteed that there will be uncomfortable times in everyone's life. I don't like using the word painful, so I say uncomfortable. Life is definitely not easy all the time no matter how firm your conviction is in your religious beliefs or how much money you possess. The best example of this is Steve Job. He had all the money in the world, but it couldn't save him or his family from feeling the pains of Cancer. Life is perfect if we see it through a spiritual prism, but not easy. Disclosing my secret to my two boys went well. I knew them well enough to know that they would be positive. Jacob, my middle child, would require a bit more information. He was intellectually curious about most things and was going to do his own research about chemotherapy and its side effects. I had a team of helpers at the house now. I was relieved it was over. Since I wasn't dead yet, and I had a new girlfriend, I decided that once my kids fall asleep, I was going to creep out and go have some adult fun. Wink Wink.

An appointment was made for me to have a PICC line (*see terms*) placed in my arm so I could get started on chemotherapy immediately. The PICC line was going to be temporary until I could have a Power Port (*see terms*) placed in my chest. The PICC line is usually inserted above the elbow into the main artery. The nurse will place this inside your arm at a regular visit. Your arm will be numbed by a local, and it usually doesn't take long at all. It doesn't hurt and requires no pain pills to recover from the procedure. You will breeze through this with no problem. The most challenging thing about having a PICC line is the dressing that is used to conceal the line and keep it clean. The dressing really bothered my skin and made it irritated. You shouldn't experience any problems and get through it easily.

While at my appointment I met an elderly lady in the lobby waiting to see her Oncologist who shared some of her experiences with chemo. We started talking, and she just finished her chemotherapy and was waiting to get her CT Scan results to know the effectiveness of her treatments. I was very curious about what to expect when I started chemo. There wasn't a book like the one I am writing that would give me some insight about what to expect that was written by patients. I knew what the doctors told me, but they have never been on the receiving end of the chemo. I always thought feedback from patients offered the best information. They knew exactly what I was going through, and frankly, I trusted them more than the doctors. The doctors mean well and are very empathetic, but they still don't have the same knowledge as a patient. Being a patient gives you the day to day experience that can only be gained if you are living through this mess. She told me that I was going to be able to tolerate it. She told me to try and stay active and positive. She also told me to drink as much water as humanly possible. There will be times when you become very fatigued and feel like you have the flu, and on those days take something for the symptoms and try to get up and keep moving. She gave me a piece of advice that I failed to follow in which I paid for after my second treatment. She told me to get adult diapers because there were a couple of times she was unable to control her bowels and pooped all over herself. She said it wasn't that bad at all, and it gave me hope that I would be able to tolerate the treatment in the same fashion.

I am going into an unknown future, but I'm still all here, still, while there's life, there's hope – John Lennon

I'm on my way to my first chemo treatment just trying to settle my nerves and any expectations about what was going to happen. I knew I had to keep present in the day that was in front of me. I didn't want to succumb to my fears. I didn't want to project bad thoughts and set myself up for failure. I knew I was battling myself as much as I was battling Cancer. I just had to do today and no more. It was a simple strategy and something I could successfully accomplish. I needed victories, no matter how small. I made dinner before I left the house so the boys can eat as soon as they get home from school. The house was clean, and all the laundry was done. I had a plan for the day, and I was ready for my first chemo treatment. MD Anderson had an outpatient clinic about 10 minutes from my house which I loved because I didn't have to go into the medical center district with all that traffic. I also didn't have to worry about parking and a long walk to get this chemo done. While at my last doctors visit they told me to expect the chemotherapy treatment would take about 6 hours. I took my prescription of Zofran (nausea medication), laptop, snacks, water, and a hoodie. As usual, I researched everything about chemotherapy so I would be prepared for entering this next phase of my journey.

I arrived at the office and proceeded over to the lab to give them blood before checking in for treatment.

You usually would have to give blood before you get started so they can make sure you are able to tolerate these toxic ass drugs they are about to pump throughout your body. In my case, it was something that they requested that I have done because of the troubles I was having with my platelet levels. They also wanted to keep an eye on my creatinine and bilirubin levels. Remember I had kidney damage because of the tacrolimus and just 9 months ago and I had my liver transplant. The oncologist was concerned that the chemo would lower my platelet levels to the point that it would be dangerous, and I would start bleeding internally. They wanted my platelet level to be at least 100. That's still low, but it would be high enough to undergo treatment. That was just another layer of concern that I had in addition to the Cancer. I had to be concerned that I may not be able to complete the treatments which in turn would leave me defenseless to the Cancer. If this were to happen, I would be put in an even worse position. There just weren't many tools left in the toolbox to combat this Cancer if chemo doesn't work. I was starting to feel like I was being backed in a corner. My dependence on a higher power was the only tool left in the box. I didn't get to stressed or obsess about it at all. It was bizarre because as I look back on it, I should have been much more concerned about the situation. Because I had been through so much already and had a dependence on God for so long it had become a comfortable during some uncomfortable times.

My labs were good, and I was given the green light to proceed with treatment. They had private rooms with these very nice lounge chairs that looked a little bigger than your conventional lounger you would find in a home and definitely more comfortable. The nurse came in and explained to me that I was getting 3 bags of medication. The first bag of medication was to help with nausea and would take about 45 minutes to complete. The next two bags would take about 5 hours to be administered. After going through the liver transplant process, it didn't take long for me to get comfortable and calm my nerves. For the last three years, I had spent so much time in doctor's offices, procedure rooms, and laying on treatment tables that it wasn't difficult for me to get mentally quiet and calm. I knew I needed something to do to keep my mind busy because if not my crazy ass mind would be racing thinking about all kinds of stuff. You have an opportunity to stop everything that is going on in your life and just sit and think. I would be lying to you if I told you the thought of dying didn't occupy space in my mind during my treatment. It wasn't to the point of obsession, but it did cross my mind. I would have to continually fight those thoughts off and focus on the good things and past miracles in my life. A grateful person is always a happy person. I was grateful for the time that I had already been given on this earth. I knew that I was fortunate and undeserving to even had made it this far. I knew I was dancing with death now that I had been diagnosed with this rare Cancer. I also knew that sooner or later the music would end, and it would be time to exit the dance floor. That's a promise that we all will fulfill at some point in our lives. We can't determine the length of the song, but we do get to choose the type of music we want to dance to while we are still on the stage. It can be a soft melody, traditional jazz, a piece by Mozart with a huge symphony, some crazy ass Rock and Roll, Rap songs expressing a type of life often misinterpreted by a broad swath of the populations, or good old soul moving Gospel music. The types of music we listen to vary as do our lifestyles. Your dance is your dance. It should be magical and arouse a good feeling when you're in the middle of the song. We are also allowed to change the music at any point in our dance with death. While sitting there getting my first chemo treatment I chose a nice ballad by someone like Adelle, thinking about all the love I have experienced, even if I got hurt in the process. Those good thoughts eventually led me to fall asleep for the last three hours of the treatment. When I did wake up, I was told that I was snoring, very loud snoring. LOL!! Shoot I was tired. I got up early and got everything knocked out at the house. I really didn't feel any different as I was driving home. Upon arrival, I took the nausea medication just to make sure I didn't get sick. Everyone was correct when they told me that the first day wouldn't be too bad at all. They also said that the worst of it will be felt the following day and as you get more and more treatments.

The first round of treatment was exactly as what I had been told by other people who have gone through chemo. I had minimal symptoms if any at all. I think I only took the nausea medication for about two days after treatment. I'm not sure if the medication was keeping me from feeling bad or the chemo drugs just weren't kicking in yet. One thing I did do was start drinking a lot more water as was suggested by the lady at met at the hospital. Just normal drinking water. Not that new space age alkaline water. Just regular water. I got up to almost a gallon a day. Drink as much as you can during your day. Try your best to at least drink half a gallon. It helped me, and it does help you flush the toxins in the chemo out of your body.

Before my second treatment, I had to go back to the hospital for a quick outpatient surgery to have a power port (*see terms*) placed in my chest. A chemotherapy port (also known as a "port-a-cath") is a small device that is implanted under your skin to allow easy access to your bloodstream. My surgery would be done by my interventional radiologist, under moderate sedation. They told me it wasn't going to take long to perform the surgery and I would be home in a couple of hours. A nurse came in and instructed me that I wouldn't be asleep for the procedure and it was relatively pain-free. The area where they will insert the port will also be numbed to ensure my comfort. I think I was starting to get too comfortable having procedures done because I fell asleep through the entire procedure. When I woke up, they were done. The nurse told me that no one has ever fallen asleep while having a port installed. She said that most people were too nervous and wanted to be awake during the procedure. I probably had got to a point where I just didn't care what they were doing as long as they hurry up and get it done so I could go. During insertion, a small triangle shaped plastic disc was placed under my skin through an inch-or-two-long incision. The port was then attached to a catheter tube that was threaded into my jugular vein near my neck and ended near the top of my heart. The recovery time was short and painless.

It was time for my second treatment, and I made sure to get there early to give blood and make sure that I was going to be medically cleared for treatment. My results came back from the labs, and my platelet count had lowered to 90. The nurse came out to instruct me that for them to proceed with my treatment they had to have approval from my oncologist. After about 30 minutes of waiting, they took me back, and we got started on the second treatment. There are always layers and impediments to fighting Cancer, so just hang in there because it's going to happen. It seemed like my chances of finishing treatment and fighting this thing were getting slimmer. You just can't keep dodging the bullet and expect not to get hit sooner or later. I was starting to doubt again. My fragile thread of hope that I worked so hard to maintain was beginning to tear apart. I knew that I had to fight off the feelings of doubt, but the reality of my circumstances, and not being fearful of the truth kept taking me back to that dark place. My will to live was still there, but I was losing some faith. I didn't realize then that one can work without the other. There will be times while fighting Cancer that we will lose some hope. If we have the will to live it will be enough to carry us during those times. Losing the will to live, but having faith just isn't possible. If the desire to carry on is absent, then there can't be faith because you will hope to die and not to live. You do not need to have faith to live, you're just hoping to die and end the suffering. I can understand when that does happen to a person fighting Cancer especially if they have been fighting for an extended period of time. It takes an emotional and physical toll after a few years. Emotionally you get tired of being disappointed after all the highs and lows that you go through. You get tired of making appointments and having your body violated. You become fatigued with having your whole life consumed with just trying to survive. We know that there will be some tough days on chemo and we will struggle. Those will be the days we fight to just keep from losing our will to live. My greatest defense has always been my children, and that's what I had to call upon to survive those days. I couldn't show weakness. I had to make sure my boys didn't see the concern and loss of hope at that moment. We are already very fragile emotionally and physically, and when any one thing is added to the equation, it can be devastating to our morale. The only thing that I had to use against all those feelings is faith. Just faith in that everything will be exactly as it is supposed to be. I had to fly above this, despite me having a broken wing, I had to fly again. I was able to get myself back together before my treatment ended. I had to get ready for the physical battle that the chemo will have on me. I remembered what everyone told me that the second treatment will be more difficult than the first. As I was driving home, I didn't feel the same as I did after the first treatment. I was starting to become nauseous on my short ride home. My middle son, Jacob, called me and asked what we are going to have for dinner. I told you when they get home from school those boys are hungry and will start looking at me crazy if they don't see any food on the oven. I told him I woke up late and didn't get a chance to prepare anything yet. I informed him that I was about 10 minutes away and would start cooking when I got home. He asked me how I was feeling after chemo. I was honest with him and told him that this time it was a little rougher than the first chemo treatment. He told me to don't worry about making dinner because he could do it for me. I jokingly said, "Boy don't burn down the house." Once I did arrive at the house, he was in the kitchen making a pasta dish of chicken and parmesan cheese in a lemon butter sauce. I asked him where he learned to cook that dish. Jacob told me that he has been watching me make that dish for over two years. Then he told me to sit my old ass down and rest. From where I was sitting I was able to watch him in the kitchen just doing his thing. A great feeling of accomplishment overwhelmed me as I saw my son taking care of his brothers and me. By this time, they had already started to do the laundry on their own and was doing a lot better job at keeping the house in order. I got up and went to the bathroom and just started to cry. It was payday today, and my bank account of calmness and serenity was being replenished. That was one of those moments that Cancer was making a direct deposit. I knew then that I had been doing a good job raising my sons. I had equipped them with enough skills that would allow them to survive in this world without me. Of course, we never want to leave our kids especially at such a young age, but I knew that if it did happen, I had given my son's a foundation that they could build upon. I also thought about the physician who failed to give me all the information about cholangio. Because I thought my prognosis was good my ex and I decided that the boys would move in with me. If he had told me the full story, they wouldn't have moved in, and I wouldn't be sitting in the bathroom having this beautiful moment. All things happen for a reason. What seemed to be a terrible thing ended up being the biggest blessing I got from this Cancer journey. Don't get me wrong I still believe that a physician should always give their patients full disclosure. It ended up that my kids were my reason to keep going on and never wanting to give up. They kept me active and made me keep faking it until I could make it!!

The fear of death was losing its power. I think that was the last thing that scared me about dying. I knew spiritually that I was prepared. I knew that I had been a very decent, caring and loving person. My past behaviors and ability to maintain good relationships with people were rewarding me. My ex-girlfriends getting me into MD Anderson so quickly and now seeing my sons for the first time as little men made me feel like

I had done ok in life. No amount of money can give you that sense of ease and comfort. I never thought about money, cars or great vacations. I just thought about people that I had touched in my life. However, this Cancer thing ends, I was ready. I was ready to lay there and enjoy my last two minutes of my life if that was my fate. It's what I always worked for my entire life. I always told people that I am living my entire life for the last two minutes of my life. I wanted to be able to lay in that bed knowing I was about to die and be able to smile knowing that I had lived a purposeful life. That day I could see that I was going to get what I always wanted from life. I knew then that the chase was over. Cancer just gave me the biggest reward ever.

I woke up the next morning feeling a bit sluggish with a terrible headache. I got up early like always and started making breakfast and dinner before getting ready to work. I started working at my friend's restaurant as a cashier to stay active for about a month or so before starting chemo. I wasn't feeling my best, but I needed to go in that day for about 4 or 5 hours. On my way to work, I felt my stomach starting to get a little bubbly. If you're a Cancer patient, you understand the term "bubble guts." LOL, As I got closer, I started to have the feeling that I needed to have a bowel movement. It came on me so fast, and I started feeling that I wasn't going to make to work in time to use the bathroom. I thought about that lady who told me that I needed to get some adult diapers before I started my chemo sessions. As I pulled up to work and before I could get out of my car, I couldn't hold it, and it just went everywhere. I could feel it dripping done my leg before I could make it out of my car. I called one of the girls inside, and she brought me a towel so I could cover my backside so everyone inside wouldn't see that I just pooped in my pants. I finally made it inside and got myself cleaned up enough that I could drive back home to shower and get a change of clothes. I called my friend Mike to tell him what happened, and to ensure him that I will be back to work after I get cleaned up. That day was a turning point for me. Game on Cancer, Game on. I got to a place that I was just sick and tired of being sick and tired. I was tired of just about everything. I became more determined than ever before that I was not going to be defeated. My will and faith were no longer going to be chipped away by this whole Cancer thing. There was nothing in this world that could break me. Nothing. The day before in the bathroom cemented my spiritual presence and today I vowed that Cancer wasn't going deter me just because my physical side was struggling. I became more grateful than ever before about what I had been given so far in my life. Being grateful became my fuel to power me through these tough times. There were days in the past that I didn't make it a priority to sit and think about my whole life, and how far I had traveled to get to this point. I made it something I did daily. My first thought every morning before my feet could hit the ground was to think about another day with my kids. Before all of my doubts and fears could come rushing at me, I made sure that I shielded myself against them. It works. If I didn't see my next birthday, then it was Ok. I also started using the short version of the serenity prayer more than ever before. "Fuck it." I was going to live as hard as I have ever lived before in my life. Things I loved to do I continued to do. It may take me a little longer, or I would have to do them a little differently than before, but I was going to keep moving forward. My friend who owned the restaurant let me put a stool near the cash register to make it through the day. There were times during the day I would have to sit and rest, but I was there busting my butt working harder than any another person at the restaurant. I always preached that there was nothing that I couldn't do in life. It was instilled in me at an early age that you can never let anybody outwork you. After that day I kept that idea in mind. I started to share more of my story with customers and discovered that it helped me, and it also helped them too. You never know who you will encourage because of your illness. They had things going on in their lives, and after talking to me, they realized that their shit didn't stink too badly. We all have things to be grateful for, and there are times we just need to be reminded of how good we really do have it despite having to deal with Cancer. I was going to keep pushing forward as hard as I could. I wasn't going to go out of this world on my back feeling defeated. I was going to leave this world fighting with a smile on my face. I was going to soar above all this craziness. It was who I was, and I totally embraced who I was and what I had accomplished in my life. There were several times during a normal day at work that I had would have to throw up, but I just washed my face in the bathroom and come out of there with a smile on my face ready to go.

As the third treatment approached, I was hoping and praying that my platelet levels would be high enough for me to move forward with my treatment. After giving them four vials of blood, I sat in the waiting room anxiously waiting for my name to be called. It was getting very close to my scheduled time for my treatment, and they still hadn't called my name. I knew then that there were some irregularities with my test results. After about another fifteen minutes a nurse came over and told me that I wasn't going to have treatment because my platelet levels were low. She told me the doctor wanted me to come back in two weeks to give blood and see if we could resume the chemo treatments. I was disappointed that I wasn't going to get my chemo done as scheduled. I knew that I needed the treatment if I was going to have any chance of surviving. It was totally out my hands, and there was nothing I could to change the decision by the doctor. I didn't let it rent to much space in my mind. I was disappointed, but I wasn't going to let this news send me on a downward spiral. I already cleared my day to have this chemo done, so I decided to have a fun day for me. I went to the movies and had a full bucket of buttery popcorn. It was a good day, I didn't have to share the popcorn or try and decide which movie to watch with a group of teenagers who would want to see some silly movie. I did what I wanted to do that day. There was nothing I could do so why not enjoy myself. When you find yourself feeling pretty good, and you don't have any obligations for the day, then you should do something for yourself. Or maybe you tell your caregiver to go out and let them enjoy themselves. Always remember there going thru this journey with you and they also have their good and bad days.

Those two weeks of waiting for my next chemo treatment seemed like forever. I stayed busy raising my kids, working, and late-night rendezvous over to my girlfriend's place. The one good thing with the break was that it gave me time to recoup from the first two treatments. I felt a lot better when it was time to go back to the infusion facility. Thank God the blood results were good enough for me to get my treatment done. They weren't good, but it was good enough. To keep my platelet level from falling, they decreased the amount of chemo that I would receive for this treatment. The nurse explained to me their reason for lowering the amount of chemo was because they wanted me to have some consistency with the amount of chemo in my system.

This schedule continued for the next two months. I would do one treatment and then skip a treatment. At the end of my three months, I only had four treatments out of the six that was planned. I would have to wait for a couple of weeks before it was time for me to get rescanned, but I really wasn't thinking that much would have changed because of the lack of consistency in getting my treatments done. I hoped that the tumor didn't grow or metastasize. That would be the greatest that I could hope for given the circumstances. I was scanned on a Friday and had to wait again until Monday to get results.

Sometimes the best thing that you can do is not think, not wonder, not imagine, not obsess. Just breathe and have faith that everything will work out for the best. – Unknown

While waiting for the results, I went back and started looking at my old blood work to check to see how my numbers have been fluctuating. I always looked at my blood work because I am always interested to see how my liver and kidneys are functioning. I usually would look at my creatinine, bilirubin, INR, and A1c results first. I became interested in two other tests that were performed since I started going to MD Anderson. I noticed the new tests that were being run were called CA-19 and CA-125 (*see terms*). I started doing some research about why they were running these tests and discovered that CA-19 may sometimes be ordered when a doctor suspects a bile duct obstruction. CA-125 is a Cancer antigen that has shown enough sensitivity and specificity to detect and monitor cholangiocarcinoma. In particular, the combination of these tumor markers seems to increase their efficiency in the diagnosing of cholangiocarcinoma. The blood results are usually published a day or two before the results of the CT-Scan or MRI. I noticed that my CA-19 and CA 125 numbers were falling. Start to pay attention to blood tests that your physician is running and do a little research on what information they are trying to glean. My results from my blood tests got me to start thinking that my scan results may not be as bad as I was expecting.

It was Monday and time to get the results to see if the chemo had any effects on the tumor. After about a

30 minutes a Physician's Assistant walked in asking the typical questions. I'm thinking c'mon let's get this over. She told me that my tumor was gone. WAIT!!!! What did she say? I didn't even get the full treatment of chemo, so I must have heard that wrong. She said that Cancer is one of those diseases that you never really know how the person's body will react to chemo. She told me that I would be rescanned in three months to see if it would come back. I was excited and very happy to hear the news. I tried my best not to get excited, but I couldn't contain my emotions. I knew that there was a chance that the Cancer could return, but today wasn't the day to start thinking about something that could happen three months down the road. I knew then that I was going to live longer than six to eight months which was the prognosis given to me by the doctor at the VA. I couldn't wait until I got home to share the news with my boys. I can't even imagine what it must have been like for them to wake up every day and think about how much longer they were going to have with their father. I made it home and when I did tell them the good news they were so relieved about the results. You could visually see it in their faces. We also decided that it was time to tell the youngest one about the most recent events. I made sure to tell him that we weren't trying to lie to him, but we decided as a group that we didn't tell him because we didn't want him to worry.

Life is a journey that must be traveled no matter how bad the roads and accommodations

- Oliver Goldsmith

The three months of waiting for the next scan seemed to go by pretty quickly. I tried my best not to think about the next scan, and I just enjoyed the break from having to go to appointments. The majority of days I rarely let it take up any space in my head at all. I did continue to do research and look for any new trial studies on cholangiocarcinoma. I knew that several studies were going on at that time and all of them showed some promise. I thought that if I could just hang in there long enough that the medical community would catch up and there would be some type of defense to this type of Cancer. I lived thru hepatitis C at a time that there were no cures and eventually they developed a cure, and now Hep C is no longer creating havoc in people's lives. Eventually the same will happen for Cancer. It will just take some time, and we all hope that this happens sooner than later.

As with all good things, my vacation from medical stuff came to an end, and I was back to blood draws, CT-Scans, and doctor visits. I had my blood test and scan done two days ago, and now it was time to see if this monster had resurfaced again. Dr. Shroff came into the room and shared the findings of my blood results and CT Scan. The Cancer had returned in the exact same spot. There was a bit of good news blended in with the results from the scan. One of the tests that were performed was to find out if I had a certain protein that helps Cancer become undetectable. The protein is called PDL-1. This is significant now with the advancements in immunotherapy (*see terms*). MD Anderson had a study that it was conducting with cholangiocarcinoma patients using an experimental drug for immunotherapy. Since it was a rare disease, it was challenging to find people who would be eligible for the study. The Doctor told me that she was going to discuss my case with the tumor board and give me a call next week. Most hospitals now will have a group of doctors that meet weekly and present cases. They decide collectively how to move forward in treating a patient. You only see one doctor, but there are several physicians making decisions on how to treat you.

I didn't feel anything when I left after seeing Dr. Shroff. I don't know if I was just numb or I had finally got to the point that being diagnosed with Cancer just wasn't that big of a deal. This was the third time that I was told I had Cancer. The big wow thing had gone by now. The initial shock just wasn't there anymore. I had gotten to the point that I immediately start thinking, "What's the next step." After so many years of dancing with death, it just gets old. I have been thinking about dying for years due to Cancer, and there were no new thoughts and scenarios to think about anymore. It was all about the fight. It wasn't about being defeated, it was only about the next step. I also decided that I was going to wait to tell the boys about the Cancer returning until Dr. Shroff contacted me with a plan. I wanted to give them some hope and how we were going to fight back. People, especially loved ones always follow up with the same response, "So, What's next." I knew my boys were old enough to make that connection.

Dr. Shroff called and told me that they wanted to do radiation (*see terms*) treatment. She made an appointment so that I could begin treatment immediately. She thought that I wasn't to that point yet to try a clinical trial for a drug that treats the whole body. There was also a small spot on my lung that turned out to be nothing after they did some further analysis. If the spot would have turned out to be a Cancerous tumor she would have listed me as a candidate for the trial drug. Radiation is something new that I had never experienced and as usual I had plenty of questions. After several hours of research, I became comfortable with the approach that they decided to fight this Cancer. It seemed like there weren't that many side effects and I would have an excellent chance to complete this treatment in its entirety.

I showed up for my first appointment and met my Gastrointestinal (GI) Radiation Oncologist. Dr. Holliday was the physician that was heading up the team that will be performing the radiation therapy. Dr. Holliday was exactly what I needed at this step in my Cancer battle. She was warm and had a welcoming spirit. She was very informative and engaging, besides she thought my quirky personality was amusing. Besides laughing at my corny jokes, I felt like I connected with her immediately. She explained to me that radiation works by making small breaks in the DNA inside cells. These breaks keep Cancer cells from growing and dividing and cause them to die. Nearby normal cells can also be affected by radiation, but most recover and go back to working the way they were designed. To minimize the effect radiation has on the body, the radiation is targeted only to specific points in your body. Chemotherapy treats the entire body and radiation is a targeted treatment. The radiation will not kill the cells immediately and will take a week or two for those cells that have been zapped to die. The goal is that those cells will die, and the tumor stops growing and start to shrink. In time if they get all the cells, Cancer will disappear altogether.

She escorted me into the room where they would do the setup work for the radiation treatments. They positioned me on a table and started to make a cast of my body so I would be in perfect position every time I had radiation blasted at my cancerous lymph node. The positioning had to be perfect for treatment to be effective and to keep other organs from being damaged by the radiation beams. They also made these two tiny tattoo dots to help them position the device. They target the tumor from several positions to ensure that they kill all the cells in the lymph node. When you go, expect to spend at least a couple of hours at your first appointment. They will move the cast to the radiation treatment facility to make sure it will be available at all your radiation treatments. Dr. Holliday told me the treatment will be 5 times a week for the next 6 weeks. My first thought was how much is this going to cost me in parking. Before I could figure out the expense of parking and all the walking that this was going to require she gave me a folder of information that addressed all my concerns. MD Anderson really did make this experience as easy as possible. I could tell they thought about everything so that a patient's treatment is as comfortable as possible.

On the first day of my treatment, I was a bit nervous because I didn't know exactly where I was going and what to expect from being hit with beams of radiation. When I did find the entrance to the hospital for radiation patients, I was quite relieved at the setup. They had valet people waiting for radiation patients arriving. This entrance is exclusively for radiation patients. Cool right!! It's a small entrance, and you head right into the hospital near the radiation treatment rooms. It wasn't a long walk at all to get to the treatment center. As expected the radiation is done in the basement, so it doesn't affect other patients in the hospital. They take the cast and place it on the table in the exact position as it was when they made the mold. I had to lay in the exact position as I did when they initially marked up the cast so the beams of radiation will hit the tumor. Putting you in the exact position that you were in when they set up the parameters for treatment took the longest time. They will pull a little bit here and then shift you around a little more until your body is in the exact location. Once they get started the actual treatment last about 10 minutes. They put a pair of glasses on you that will monitor your breathing. There is a green bar that measures your breathing, and you must keep that bar inside a box while they are shooting the radiation beams. As you start to hold your breath, the line keeps rising until it's in the green zone, and you must hold your breath to maintain that line position. It's not for a very long time, and then you can exhale. There was some fatigue I experienced, but nothing compared to chemo. It's a piece of cake. You got this!!

By far the hardest thing was going to the hospital and being reminded every day of the devastating effects of Cancer and the number of lives and families going through this thing. Usually, you go to the hospital once every two weeks or in some instances once a month, but when doing radiation therapy, you are there every day. You never get a chance to forget about your Cancer. You see young, old, black, white, yellow, brown, Catholic, Jewish, Christians, etcetera all going through the same thing. Everyone feels the same way and praying for the same thing. Literally, I think it is the only place that people don't care about color, religion and or political parties. No one is asking if their doctor is Pro-Life, Pro 2nd Amendment, Muslim, or even a Liberal. Trust me no one in there is bad mouthing Obama Care either. Everyone in there has pre-existing conditions that a very short time ago would of have kept quite a few people who are getting treatment from being able to get care now. Well, they would have gotten care, but they butt would be broke or in debt up to their eyeballs.

I can remember one morning when I got into the elevator with a mother and her young boy who was fighting Cancer. He must have been no older than ten. She rubbed on his head and said," I know you're tired." I did all I could do not to cry in the elevator. Just seeing death and despair every day is difficult. You see hundreds of empty vessels walking around the hospital with an empty look in their eyes. You could say that there wasn't any hope still left in them. They had given all that they had to Cancer. You want to keep your spirits up, but some days it was almost impossible. Somedays I just wanted to run away from that hospital and never come back. There was some physical fatigue from the radiation, but by far it was the emotional and spiritual fatigue with this treatment. I didn't have any problems with my platelet levels compared to going through chemo. All my blood results were spot on.

My last day of treatment ended and that always means that you get to ring the bell. They had the bell attached to the wall near the exit of the treatment offices. While waiting for your treatment, you can hear the bell ringing, and you knew someone just finished their final round of radiation. I always said a prayer for the person with the hopes that their treatment was successful. The day had arrived, and it was finally my turn to ring the bell. After treatment, I rang the bell and the whole staff came out and congratulated me on getting through my treatments. I started to exit and could hear the people in the waiting room clapping. It was magical. That feeling only lasts for a short time, but it was great. I'm sure I hugged every person in the waiting room. I was so tired of going to the hospital every day. As you're going through radiation every day, you start seeing the same people and really get to know their story. A bond is created, and you are genuinely happy for them when they finish. I felt that kinship as I walked out of that door. I wasn't sure how effective the treatment was in curing my Cancer, but I was just happy that I didn't have to return the following week. You always hope that it's your last time ringing the bell, but only time will tell. I was instructed on my last day that I had to wait six weeks before I could get scanned to get an idea if the treatments were successful. I'm back to that whole waiting game and trying not stress. If you aren't a patient person before starting on this Cancer trip, you will learn to be a patient person pretty quickly.

The six weeks went by fast, and before I knew it, I was back in that cold room with an IV in arm holding my breath getting scanned again. I don't even know how many times I have been scanned, but this one was as important as the one that got me back on the transplant list. There weren't any more tools left in the toolbox for curing my Cancer. The results from this scan will be given to me by Dr. Holliday. I was glad that she was the one I would see for a couple of reasons. First, she was always on time and two, she was excellent at explaining what she saw in the scan. I got checked in to see the doctor and was taken back immediately to get my vitals done before getting my results. I wasn't in the room five minutes before Dr. Holliday arrived with two interns. I joked with her as usual and then it was time to get down to business. She told me that everything looked good and it looked as if the Cancer was gone. There was a spot on the image in the exact location where the lesion was previously, but she said it looked like it was just scarring from radiation. She told me that she was pretty sure everything was okay and would rescan me again in three months.

That's been over a year and a half ago, and the six scans I have had since completing my radiation have been clean. I asked the Doctor how long it will be before I can feel like I'm out of danger of it returning. He said about five years. He also said that the odds get better that Cancer won't return as more time passes. I know that it can return at any time and the whole process can start all over with just one lousy scan. I will always have to monitor my myself because of the liver transplant and other medical conditions, but it won't have the same intensity as I experienced knowing I was dancing with death. Death will always be out there for all of us, but today I'm not on the dance floor. I'm on the sidelines watching and listening to the music.

What lies behind us and what lies before us are tiny matters compared to what lies within us

-Ralph Waldo Emerson

When I look back at the whole experience, I am just blown away at what I went through to get to this point. It was a series of 24 hours that were strung together to be able to survive this journey. I was able to grow to be a better and more understanding person. As much as I wanted doctors to be God like I learned that they have good and bad days too. They are humans and make errors in judgment just like the rest of us. It's our responsibility to be active participants in our healthcare. We must try and learn as much as we can about our disease. Cancer is a mystery to us and equally as baffling to doctors. There is so much more that must be learned about how to combat this illness. Medicine is making great strides today, so we must try and hold on. Physicians who treat Cancer patients are very special people and deserve a lot of thanks because it's not easy. They are often treating people who are very sick and depends on them to save their lives. What a responsibility to carry around every day. That's difficult because I have learned that a person's body type and gene makeup will react to treatments differently. I was given a death sentence, and for some reason, my body reacted very well to radiation treatment. So please just hang in there and keep fighting. A perfectly healthy person somewhere in this world will die today and won't have a chance to say their goodbye's. We have a chance to do so, and we should take full advantage of that blessing. Love as hard and as often as you can while you can. God Bless.

Glossary of Terms

Transplant Surgery - Organ transplantation is a medical procedure in which an organ is removed from one body and placed in the body of a recipient, to replace a damaged or missing organ. The donor and recipient may be at the same location, or organs may be transported from a donor site to another location. Organs and/or tissues that are transplanted within the same person's body are called autografts. Transplants that are recently performed between two subjects of the same species are called allografts. Allografts can either be from a living or cadaveric source.

AFP- Increased AFP levels may indicate the presence of cancer, most commonly liver cancer, cancer of the ovary, or germ cell tumor of the testicles. However, not every liver, ovarian, or testicular cancer will produce significant quantities of AFP.

Elevated levels may sometimes be seen with other cancers such as stomach, colon, lung, breast, and lymphoma, although it is rarely ordered to evaluate these conditions. Other diseases such as cirrhosis and hepatitis can also cause increased levels. When AFP is used as a monitoring tool, decreasing levels indicate a response to treatment. If concentrations after cancer treatment do not significantly decrease, usually to normal or near normal levels, then some of the tumor tissue may still be present.

Jaundice- is the medical term that describes yellowing of the skin and eyes. Jaundice itself is not a disease, but it is a symptom of several possible underlying illnesses. Jaundice forms when there is too much bilirubin in your system. Bilirubin is a yellow pigment that is created by the breakdown of dead red blood cells in the liver. Normally, the liver gets rid of bilirubin along with old red blood cells. It's one symptom of a failing liver.

eGFR-is short for estimated glomerular filtration rate. Your eGFR is a number based on your blood test for creatinine, a waste product in your blood. It tells how well your kidneys are working. A normal eGFR is 60 or more. If your eGFR is less than 60 for three months or more, your kidneys may not be working well. If your eGFR is below 15, you may need to start dialysis or have a kidney transplant.

ALT &AST - If the liver is injured or damaged, the liver cells spill these enzymes into the blood, raising the AST and ALT enzyme blood levels and signaling liver disease.

CBC - This test is used to assess a patient's overall health. CBC tests are very common and can indicate abnormalities in the blood or in any particular part of the body, including the liver. CBC tests count the number of red blood cells, white blood cells, and platelets as well as the amount of hemoglobin found in the blood.

Creatinine - The kidneys maintain the blood creatinine in a normal range. Creatinine has been found to be a reliable indicator of kidney function. Elevated creatinine level signifies impaired kidney function or kidney disease.

Bilirubin- A bilirubin test measures how much bilirubin is in the blood. Bilirubin is made when red blood cells break down. The liver changes the bilirubin so that it can be excreted from the body. High bilirubin levels might mean there's a problem with the liver. This one the most important tests because it is used in determining your MELD Score.

PT/INR- The prothrombin time (PT) is a test that helps evaluate a person's ability to appropriately form blood clots. The international normalized ratio or INR is a calculation based on the results of a PT that is used to monitor individuals who are being treated with the blood-thinning medication.

CT Scan – A computed tomography (CT or CAT) scan allows doctors to see inside your body. It uses a combination of X-rays and a computer to create pictures of your organs, bones, and other tissues. It shows more detail than a regular X-ray.

MRI – An MRI (or magnetic resonance imaging) scan is a radiology technique that uses magnetism, radio waves, and a computer to produce images of body structures. The MRI scanner is a tube surrounded by a giant circular magnet. The patient is placed on a moveable bed that is inserted into the magnet. The magnet creates a strong magnetic field that aligns the protons of hydrogen atoms, which are then exposed to a beam of radio waves. This spins the various protons of the body, and they produce a faint signal that is detected by the receiver portion of the MRI scanner. The receiver information is processed by a computer, and an image is produced. The image and resolution produced by MRI are quite detailed and can detect tiny changes of structures within the body. For some procedures, contrast agents, such as gadolinium, are used to increase the accuracy of the images.

Encephalopathy - Symptoms, and signs of moderate hepatic encephalopathy may include difficulty thinking, personality changes, poor concentration, problems with handwriting or loss of other small-hand movements, confusion, forgetfulness, poor judgment, a musty or sweet breath odor. Symptoms of severe hepatic encephalopathy are confusion, drowsiness or lethargy, anxiety, seizures, severe personality changes, fatigue, confused speech, shaky hands, and slow movements. I experienced some signs of encephalopathy while waiting for my liver transplant.

Ascites- Ascites is the accumulation of fluid (usually

serous fluid which is a pale yellow and clear fluid) that accumulates in the abdominal (peritoneal) cavity. It looks like the patients are severely bloated. The most common cause of ascites is advanced liver disease or cirrhosis. Although the exact mechanism of ascites development is not completely understood, most theories suggest portal hypertension (increased pressure in the liver blood flow to the liver) as the main contributor.

Hear Catheterization – Cardiac catheterization is a medical procedure used to diagnose and treat some heart conditions. A long, thin, flexible tube called a catheter is put into a blood vessel in your arm, groin (upper thigh), or neck and threaded to your heart. Through the catheter, your doctor can do diagnostic tests and treatments on your heart.

For example, your doctor may put a special type of dye into the catheter. The dye will flow through your bloodstream to your heart. Then, your doctor will take x-ray pictures of your heart. The dye will make your coronary (heart) arteries visible on the pictures. This test is called coronary angiography. The dye can show whether a waxy substance called plaque (plak) has built up inside your coronary arteries. Plaque can narrow or block the arteries and restrict blood flow to your heart. The buildup of plaque in the coronary arteries is called coronary heart disease (CHD) or coronary artery disease.

Doctors also can use ultrasound during cardiac catheterization to see blockages in the coronary arteries. Ultrasound uses sound waves to create detailed pictures of the heart's blood vessels. Doctors may take samples of blood and heart muscle during cardiac catheterization or do minor heart surgery. Cardiologists (heart specialists) usually do cardiac catheterization in a hospital. You're awake during the procedure, and it causes little or no pain. However, you may feel some soreness in the blood vessel where the catheter was inserted. Cardiac catheterization rarely causes serious complications.

PET Scan – Positron emission tomography (PET) is a nuclear imaging technique that creates detailed, computerized pictures of organs and tissues inside the body.

A PET scan reveals how the body is functioning and uncovers areas of abnormal metabolic activity. During a PET scan, the patient is first injected with a glucose (sugar) solution that contains a very small amount of radioactive material. The substance is absorbed by the organs or tissues being examined. The patient rests on a table and slides into a large tunnel-shaped scanner. The PET scanner is then able to "see" damaged or Cancerous cells where the glucose is being taken up (Cancer cells often use more glucose than normal cells) and the rate at which the tumor is using the glucose (which can help determine the tumor grade). The procedure is painless and varies in length, depending on the part of the body that is being evaluated. A PET scan can be used to detect Cancerous tissues and cells in the body that may not always be found through computed tomography (CT) or magnetic resonance imaging (MRI).

Endoscopy- With the procedure known as gastrointestinal endoscopy, a doctor can see the inside lining of your digestive tract. This examination is performed using an endoscope-a flexible fiber-optic tube with a tiny TV camera at the end. The camera is connected to either an eyepiece for direct viewing or a video screen that displays the images on a color TV. The endoscope not only allows diagnosis of gastrointestinal (GI) disease but treatment as well.

Colonoscopy - Colonoscopy is a procedure that enables an examiner (usually a gastroenterologist) to evaluate the inside of the colon (large intestine or large bowel). The colonoscope is a four-foot long, flexible tube about the thickness of a finger with a camera and a source of light at its tip. The tip of the colonoscope is inserted into the anus and then is advanced slowly, under visual control, into the rectum, and through the colon usually as far as the cecum, which is the first part of the colon.

TACE –Transarterial Chemo Embolization therapy involves administration of chemotherapy directly to the liver tumor via a catheter. With this technique, the chemotherapy targets the tumor while sparing the patient many side effects of traditional chemotherapy that is given to the whole body. Following chemotherapy, your physician will embolize (cut off) the blood supply to the tumors. In this manner, the tumor is treated using two different techniques. If necessary, TACE can be performed multiple times to achieve the desired response in the tumor.

CA 125 - Is a protein that is a so-called tumor marker or biomarker, which is a substance that is found in greater concentration in tumor cells than in other cells of the body. In particular, CA 125 is present in greater concentration in ovarian Cancer cells than in other cells. It was first identified in the early 1980s, and the function of the CA 125 protein is not currently understood. CA stands for Cancer antigen. CA 125 is often measured as a blood test.

CA-19-9 -The marker is measured in the blood of an individual. Generally speaking, as the disease advances, it will produce greater ca-19-9 elevation. Therefore, the CA-19-9 blood test is useful to detect the presence of the condition as well as to detect how far the condition has advanced. The substance CA-19-9 is produced by the gland when it is affected by Cancer. Under normal circumstances, there will be some small amount of CA-19-9 in the blood. When this value rises, the doctor will suspect pancreatic Cancer. Some studies have also shown that colon Cancer may be detected similarly, although there are other tests for colon Cancer that are more specific and, therefore, more accurate.

Radiation – Radiation therapy uses high-energy particles or waves, such as x-rays, gamma rays, electron beams, or protons, to destroy or damage Cancer cells.

Your cells normally grow and divide to form new cells. But Cancer cells grow and divide faster than most normal cells. Radiation works by making small breaks in the DNA inside cells. These breaks keep Cancer cells from growing and dividing and cause them to die. Nearby normal cells can also be affected by radiation, but most recover and go back to working the way they should. Unlike chemotherapy, which usually exposes the whole body to Cancer-fighting drugs, radiation therapy is usually a local treatment. In most cases, it's aimed at and affects only the part of the body being treated. Radiation treatment is planned to damage Cancer cells, with as little harm as possible to nearby healthy cells.

Chemotherapy – Chemotherapy is a drug treatment that uses powerful chemicals to kill fast-growing cells in your body. Chemotherapy is most often used to treat Cancer since Cancer cells grow and multiply much more quickly than most cells in the body. Many different chemotherapy drugs are available. Chemotherapy drugs can be used alone or in combination to treat a wide variety of Cancers. Though chemotherapy is an effective way to treat many types of Cancer, chemotherapy treatment also carries a risk of side effects. Some chemotherapy side effects are mild and treatable, while others can cause serious complications.

Immunotherapy - Immunotherapy is a broad category of Cancer therapies that use the body's immune system to fight Cancer cells. These cells are different from normal cells, in that they do not die normally. Think of these rapidly-dividing cells like an out-of-control copy machine that won't stop creating images. These abnormal cells frequently change, or "mutate," to evade the immune system. Immunotherapy drugs are designed to alert the immune system about these mutated cells so it can locate and destroy them.

The immune system is always on patrol, like a police force charged with ridding the body of foreign invaders, such as viruses, bacteria or fungi. Lymph nodes, which make up most of the immune system, serve as police stations throughout the body. White blood cells, such as "T cells," fight infection and Cancer. They are the police officers. When a foreign invader is detected, the entire immune system is alerted through chemical signals, just as a police station would radio police officers to alert them to a problem.

Cancer cells are not recognized as invaders because

they are the body's own cells that have mutated so that once-healthy cells no longer behave like normal cells. The immune system doesn't recognize this distinction, allowing these dangerous cells to grow, divide and spread throughout the body. One way Cancerous cells stay hidden is by sending signals to the PD-1 CTLA-4 receptors at certain checkpoints on immune cells. Those signals trick the body's police force into thinking the Cancer cells are normal. Immunotherapy drugs known as checkpoint inhibitors are designed to disrupt those signals, allowing the Cancer cells to be exposed as invaders and triggering an immune system response. Cytokines and Cancer vaccines are other types of immunotherapies used to generate an immune response by helping the body recognize Cancer cells.

PICC Lines - (Peripherally inserted central catheter) The Picc line goes into a vein in your arm, under local anesthetic. A doctor or nurse can put it in during an outpatient appointment. The line runs up the vein inside your arm and ends up in a large vein in your chest. You can have chemotherapy and other drugs and fluids through a PICC line. PICC lines can be left in for several months and used in a similar way to other central lines. The line is flushed regularly with heparin (an anti-clotting drug) or salt water (saline) to clean the line and prevent clotting.

Chemotherapy Port - A port consists of a reservoir compartment (the portal) that has a silicone bubble for needle insertion (the septum), with an attached plastic tube (the catheter). The device is surgically inserted under the skin in the upper chest or in the arm and appears as a bump under the skin. It requires no special maintenance and is completely internal, so swimming and bathing are not a problem. The catheter runs from the portal and is surgically inserted into a vein (usually the jugular vein or less optimally the subclavian vein). Ideally, the catheter terminates in the superior vena cava or the right atrium. This position allows infused agents to be spread throughout the body quickly and efficiently. The implantation procedure itself is considered minor and is typically performed with both local anesthesia and moderate sedation. Patients often have post-procedure discomfort at the insertion site which is most often managed by administration of acetaminophen or a non-steroidal anti-inflammatory drug such as ibuprofen.

A port is most commonly inserted as an outpatient surgery procedure in a hospital or clinic by an interventional radiologist or surgeon, under moderate sedation. Implantation is increasingly performed by interventional radiologists due to advancements in techniques and their facile use of imaging technologies. When no longer needed, the port can be removed in the interventional radiology suite or an operating room.

Radiation Therapy - Radiation therapy (also called radiotherapy) is a Cancer treatment that uses high doses of radiation to kill Cancer cells and shrink tumors. At low doses, radiation is used in x-rays to see inside your body, as with x-rays of your teeth or broken bones. At high doses, radiation therapy kills Cancer cells or slows their growth by damaging their DNA. Cancer cells whose DNA is damaged beyond repair stop dividing or die. When the damaged cells die, they are broken down and removed by the body.

Radiation therapy does not kill Cancer cells right away. It takes days or weeks of treatment before DNA is damaged enough for Cancer cells to die. Then, Cancer cells keep dying for weeks or months after radiation therapy ends.

If you have any questions or comments contact me at eugenebrooks@fcancernow.com. Please visit my website for additional information. www.fcancernow.com

www.ingramcontent.com/pod-product-compliance
Lightning Source LLC
LaVergne TN
LVHW051519070426
835507LV00023B/3191